Who has House !!

Your Buddy
Pris

CAT TALK!

Cover Illustration by Peter Warner
(www.peterwarner.co.uk)
Interior Design by Janice L. Marchant

CONTENTS

By Suzanne Smither
with Cleo, Faith and Hope Smither

In loving memory of Leo and Merlin

INTRODUCTION

Cats are creatures of myth and mystery. Are they aloof and self-sufficient, or affectionate and sociable? Do they love us or do they keep us around just for the food and shelter?

Can they see in the dark, see colors, see into the future? Do they communicate with their tails? Can their whiskers really forecast the weather? Do kitties from the pound make the best pets? Are wild cats dangerous? Can they be tamed?

Then there are the puzzles of daily life: Is it better to be an only cat or part of a multi-cat household? What should you feed your cat, and how often? What are the best toys? Should the cat or the human be expected to fetch? How many litter boxes does a prissy puss need? Kitty, how do you make sure you get the best perch or napping spot? Is there a remedy for unsightly furballs? How do you train your human to lie still if you're sleeping on him or her? Owner, can you train your cat to go peacefully when it's time to visit the vet?

The authors of this book, three brilliant cats and a reasonably intelligent woman with more than 20 years experience as a companion to cats, answer all these questions. We also share communication techniques, cat etiquette, feline astrology and much more to help foster understanding between felines and folks.

SHARING YOUR LIFE WITH A CAT

I f you're about to live with a cat for the first time, you must wonder which comes closer to the truth – the many cat lovers who describe felines as bright, beautiful, purring angels who fill human lives with joy, or horror stories about aloof beasts who ignore people completely, except when complaining about the food or soiling the carpet in protest of some imagined wrong.

While I never met a cat I didn't like, truthfulness compels me to admit that few kitties are flawless. The characters of most are neither black nor white, but shaded with the countless hues of gray in between – along with tabby stripes, leopard spots, Siamese points and calico patches.

Before you can form a mutually satisfying relationship with your kitty, you need to develop the proper *cat*-titude. Students of Zen have a head start.

A Cat Is Not a Human

I bet you don't have many human friends who greet you by rubbing their cheeks against your feet, kneading your underarms or "mooning" you – yet these are traditional greetings practiced by even the most refined felines.

8

The foot-rub allows your cat to savor that irresistible *eau-de-toe* while depositing a scent from his facial glands that marks you as his personal property. Your armpits, even when freshly bathed and deodorized, have a fragrance that reminds him of happy moments as a nursing kitten. And when your cat presents his bottom, tail up, at close range, he's mimicking another behavior from early kittenhood, when Momcat lined her little ones up for daily inspection and cleaning.

You'll know you're loved when your kitty rubs her head against you, lies on you, purrs loudly in your presence or looks straight at you while squeezing her eyes contentedly. You can let her know you feel the same by scratching her special spot (try behind the ears, under the chin, between the shoulder blades or at the base of the tail), squeezing your eyes slowly and blinking, offering catnip or giving her a back and neck rub.

Cats are creatures of great dignity and uniqueness, not to be confused with babies, children or ornery in-laws, despite certain startling resemblance to all of the above. While some cats love to be cuddled and cooed over, others would rather forfeit a lobster dinner than submit to even a short petting session.

My household contains three feline divas with distinct personalities:

Cleo is a chocolate point Siamese princess, adopted from a cattery of champions at the age of eight weeks.

Hope was rescued from dire circumstances as a critically ill, three-month-old feral kitten. (Feral is a term used for cats, like Hope's parents, who may once have been pets, but have been on their own so long that they turned semi-wild.)

Faith, Hope's healthy littermate, camped out on the

9

patio for months until I, impoverished by Hope's stay in intensive care, could afford another trip to the vet for shots, flea dip and ear mite treatment.

Blue-eyed, brunette Cleo, who looks like Audrey Hepburn in mink, runs the household with a flick of her velvet paw (which sometimes lands with a thud on the nose of a feline roommate who needs to be reminded who's boss). Yet she drops her regal pose whenever I'm around.

An extreme example of an unusually affectionate breed, Cleo loves to play Velcro Cat, clinging to my knees by night, claiming my lap by day, and generally going out of her way to let me know I'm "kneaded." If she thinks I'm too wrapped up in my work, she'll walk back and forth across my computer keyboard, leap onto a bookcase and knock a few volumes to the floor, or sit at my feet and scold me until I give her my undivided attention.

Hope, born in the woods near my home to a Siamese mother and a (mostly) Maine Coon father, is a hefty armful of gray and white fluff, with sparkling gold eyes, a winning smile and an awesome array of whiskers. She greets new humans, new animals and new situations with friendly curiosity. Her attitude seems to be "the more the merrier, as long as the food bowl is full."

This fearless survivor loves to cuddle and can play for hours on end. She drapes herself over my computer monitor and swats the cards in the solitaire game, and comes to the phone to offer purrs and kisses when she knows "Grandma" is on the line. Highly sociable, she's also self-reliant enough to find her own fun when everyone else is busy.

Faith, Hope's half-sister, is a shy, green-eyed beauty in a sleek, gunmetal-gray coat. She inherited much of her personality from her father, a stealthy black panther-lookalike who prowls the neighborhood by night. Her looks and sweet temperament suggest she has Russian Blue in her family tree.

When she first joined our family, Faith was a touch-me-not who'd duck under the bed at the slightest unfamiliar sound or movement. It took her two years to gradually emerge from her shell. Now she'll let me stroke her back, rub her tummy or return her special greeting, a head-butt accompanied by a loud purr. Still, she's shyer than the other girls and disappears when company comes. Her favorite pastime is making midnight watch-cat patrols, which end with long sessions in a high window where she can see what the neighbors are up to.

The differences in my pusses' personalities are due partly to heredity and partly to their early experiences with their feline families and with humans. We'll explore this subject further in Chapter 2, about the do's and don'ts of adoptions and rescues.

Mark Twain summed it up perfectly when he said, "If man were to be crossed with the cat, it would greatly improve man, but deteriorate the cat."

Banishing Harmful Myths

Now that you've decided to adopt that sweet kitten you saw at the shelter or formalize your casual relationship with the lovable stray you've been feeding at the back door, you need to learn all the facts you can about cat care – and fast. Unfortunately, many of them are buried under piles of phooey masquerading as common knowledge. Here are some of the worst cat myths I've heard, and the truth behind the misconceptions.

Myth: *There's no reason to neuter or spay. In order to be well-adjusted, male cats need to roam and enjoy sex, and females need to have kittens.*

Truth: These are some of the biggest mistruths ever to circulate the globe. What was natural for our pets' wild ancestors is downright dangerous for today's house-cats. Unless a kitty is earmarked for a breeding program, eliminating his or her ability to reproduce does your animal a great favor. It can even be a lifesaver.

A neutered male loses his desire to mate and most of his desire to roam. He becomes more people-oriented and is less likely to spray his strong scent around the house. Content at home, he's safe from cars, cat fights, animal abusers and a host of irritants, including fleas, ticks and ear mites, poison plants and chemicals, toads, snakes and skin fungus. And he tends to live longer.

The benefits of spaying are just as great for the female. Instead of experiencing the extreme mood swings of estrus (going into heat) several times a year, she's relaxed and even-tempered, focusing on her humans rather than the suitors outside. If spayed before her first heat, she's also far less likely to develop tumors later in life. And, like the male, she avoids all those outdoor hazards.

When you spay or neuter your cat, you're also doing your community a favor by helping to ease the severe pet overpopulation problem. If you wonder what harm it can possibly do to bring a few more kittens into the world, consider this: A breeding pair that produces just one litter of four kittens could actually swell the feline population by 262,144 over the next eight years. That's assuming each of those kittens is a female who grows up and gives birth each year to four female kittens of her own, who grow up to do the same (a conservative estimate, since many roaming females have two or three litters a year). Replace even a few hundred of those hypothetical female kittens with wide-ranging, promiscuous toms, and the figures go from staggering to downright incomprehensible.

By the way, those stories you hear about altered cats becoming fat and lazy are just more nonsense. A few eventually become obese because of their genes or medical conditions, but most, given a healthful diet and adequate exercise, weigh within the normal range for their breed, age and sex. If your tabby. getting tubby, it's probably nothing you can't remedy with smaller portions and longer play periods.

If you're a caring cat companion, the question is not whether to neuter or spay, but when. Six months of age has been the standard for many years, but a number of veterinarians now believe it's best to perform these procedures even earlier. Ask a vet you trust.

Myth: *Keeping a cat indoors all the time is cruel and unnatural.*

Truth: It's the other way around. Letting cats fend for themselves outside, even for a few hours a day, exposes them to a host of dangers and diseases.

If you can provide a backyard free of harmful plants, with trees for climbing, surrounded by a 10-foot fence, your cat will have the best of both worlds. But he or she can enjoy a long, happy life without ever setting a paw outdoors. A puss offered plenty of perches, scratching posts, windowsills, napping spots and toys won't wonder about the outdoor life, because what's going on inside is just fine.

If you want to let your cat experience the outdoors safely and have enough space, you can construct a screened-in run that allows access to sunshine, fresh air and the sights and smells of nature. Or you can buy a manufactured kitty condo that offers similar benefits. If you're a city dweller with limited space, don't fret. A screened balcony or window box can provide plenty of safe thrills.

Myth: *I don't have to worry about the cat scratching the couch. I'll declaw the cat.*

Truth: People who care more about furniture than living creatures have no business adopting cats in the first place.

A cat without its front claws has virtually no defense against the fierce animals and abusive humans it might meet if it ever wandered away from home.

Declawing is a serious surgical procedure that requires general anesthesia. It involves removing each nail along with its attached bone. If the procedure is bungled, infection, deformity or even permanent crippling can result.

Even if a cat makes it through declawing without great pain or frustration and is kept strictly indoors, it could still be at a disadvantage later in life. If the people who had him declawed were ever unable to care for him, he'd have a harder time being adopted, because it wouldn't

14

be fair to place him in a home with cats or dogs that have their claws. (I've turned down cats I might otherwise have adopted, for exactly this reason.)

Humane alternatives include trimming your cat's claws regularly, and, if scratching is a problem, applying inexpensive plastic claw caps. Available from veterinarians, these come in a range of sizes and snazzy colors. They're attached with an adhesive like fingernail glue, and can be replaced every month or so as the claws grow out.

If you decorate with denim (fur-resistant, virtually indestructible and always in fashion), cut velvet (luxurious, durable and paw-repellent), canvas, tapestry or other hardy fabrics without a vertical weave, and provide a scratching post or pad, you can probably persuade the cat to leave your things alone.

Even a persistent couch-shredder can usually be weaned from destructive behavior by spraying the furniture with cat repellent, sprinkling it with "not-here-kitty" herbs or placing a can full of pennies where it's sure to fall and make a loud noise at the first approach of a paw.

I realize my feelings on this subject are extreme. In fairness, it must be said that many humane veterinarians do declaw felines if it will improve their chances of being adopted as house cats or remaining in the homes they already have.

Myth: *Cats are loners, so it won't matter if my pet is home alone all day while I work.*

Truth: Although they can be quite self-reliant when necessary, most cats are social creatures who need lots of attention and affection and shouldn't be left by themselves too long. If your job keeps you away from home for most of the day, consider adopting two kitties so they can keep each other company.

Myth: *Cats and dogs are natural enemies who could never get along as pets in the same family.*

Truth: Many cats are contented members of households where dogs, rabbits, hamsters, gerbils, birds, fish, turtles or iguanas are also in residence. In fact, some count dogs, rabbits or horses as their best buddies.

The only real objections to mixing the species are based on common sense. You wouldn't ask a kitten to live with a pit bull who's been trained to kill, or a large snake who views smaller mammals as lunch.

Companion animals should be introduced to each other gradually, with the newcomer confined to a single room for a few weeks so the current pets can become familiar with its scent and sounds. Then they can all meet face to face for increasingly longer periods each day. If the older pets are given extra affection and reassurance, and all the animals can see that there's plenty of love, food and space to go around, they usually accept and learn to like each other. Territorial disputes may arise, but that can happen among members of the same species, too. Ask anyone who's raised a pair of toddlers.

Myth: *It's not safe to let the cat near your baby. He will suck the breath from the infant.*

Truth: This is a superstition that probably dates back to medieval times when cats were considered to be evil spirits. Most cats aren't interested in babies. Those who are want nothing more than to cuddle with someone soft and warm who's about their size.

However, no cat (or any animal) should ever be left alone with a baby. In his attempt to cuddle or play with the child, he may accidentally smother him or her. If the cat and infant are introduced gradually, they should get along fine, provided their play sessions are brief and monitored by adults.

Myth: *Only a purebred kitten from a reputable breeder (or a mixed-breed cat from a shelter) will do.*

Truth: There's no one-size-fits-all answer here. It takes a lot of thought and research to decide what sort of puss is best for you, whether you should choose a kitten or an older cat, and where you should go to adopt your new companion.

It's worth the effort, because the right kitty can become a cherished family member for a long time to come. Advances in nutrition and veterinary care have lengthened cats' lifespans from around eight years to the teens and beyond, assuming their humans care for them properly and keep them indoors. Many cats now live to celebrate their twentieth birthdays (that's almost one hundred in people years!). The longest-lived cat on record was thirty-four; the oldest cat show competitor I know of is still winning ribbons at twenty-seven.

Myth: *Don't bother trying to rescue feral cats. They're impossible to tame and can never make satisfactory pets.*

Truth: "Phooey," say Hope and Faith. "YOU try being constantly on the run from dogs, kids, raccoons and possums, climbing trees to seek shelter from the rain, and making do with lizard gizzards when your mouth is watering for turkey breast. We're thrilled to be living indoors. Now that we're house cats, the view from the window is all the nature we need."

ADOPTIONS AND RESCUES

Cats come into our lives in a variety of ways: purebred adoptions that are as eagerly anticipated (and almost as expensive) as the birth of a child, casual "Mom, look who followed me home" arrangements, love-at-first-sight matches at animal shelters, and emergencies that compel anyone with a heart to rescue a feline in trouble.

With enough love and patience, any of these can be the first step toward a wonderful, lasting puss/person relationship. But as with any important commitment, there are things that can go wrong. Taking the time to decide what kind of cat is best for you, then sticking to your decision, can help you avoid many of them. Knowing your legal rights as an adopter or rescuer can help you avoid many more.

FINDING YOUR IDEAL CAT

Your ideal cat may be a purebred kitten, an older cat adopted from a shelter, a homeless waif who adopts you or a pampered feline you fall for at a cat show.

How can you be sure which sort of cat would make the best companion for you? First of all, take an inventory of your living space and lifestyle. Cats can adapt to

19

any environment from a studio apartment to a farm, but generally speaking, the gentler, less active breeds do best in small spaces, while the livelier, more athletic types need more room to romp and space to explore.

It's possible to keep a "hyper" cat happy in an apartment, but in order to do so, you'll need to provide plenty of interesting cat furniture and make the most of vertical as well as horizontal space. If you'd prefer a cat who'll just curl up for a nap on the couch you already have, choose one of the more mellow breeds or a middle-aged cat rather than a kitten.

Consider the people and pets you live with, too. A cat that would do fine with an older couple might be intimidated by an active family with four kids and two dogs.

Purebreds

A purebred kitten may cost from a hundred to thousands of dollars, depending on the rarity of the breed and the supply and demand in your area. It's a worthwhile investment if you're smitten by the looks and personality of a certain breed.

A major advantage of purebreds is that they tend to conform in looks and temperament to others who share their bloodlines. While individuals can have strikingly different personalities, basic breed characteristics are fairly predictable.

For example, Cleo tells what to expect if you adopt one of the most popular shorthairs, a Siamese:

"We're very bright, so please take time to join us in challenging games. We're happy to act as personal trainers by scaling the drapes or perching on the refrigerator so you can climb after us. Children are some of our favorite playmates because they have almost as much energy as we do.

"We love to chat with people and other cats – once in a while we even sing opera. We'll also help you work, cook or read. We follow our favorite humans everywhere, even into the shower. In bed, we make perfect heating pads for aching shoulders or knees.

"We're one-person cats who form strong attachments and can't help being a little *paw*ssessive of those we love. Please excuse the occasional display of jealousy. We actually get along quite well with other family members and friends, as long as you remember to give us lots of hugs and tell us how special we are. Feline roommates are okay if they promise to be our loyal subjects."

The rule of "paw" about cat breeds is that slender shorthairs like Abyssinians and Cornish Rexes are generally smarter, more curious and more active, while plump longhairs like Persians and Ragdolls tend to be less intellectual, more relaxed and more agreeable about grooming sessions, which they require daily.

Most purebreds are affectionate, but some bond with one individual while others prefer to hang out with the whole family. They also differ in their degree of tolerance for other cats, dogs, children, company, noises and large groups of people.

Unlike cats of unknown parentage who can change radically from kittenhood to adulthood, purebreds provide few surprises as they develop. Look at a six-month-old kitten and you'll have a good idea of how the full-grown cat will look and act.

But genes don't count for everything. A bad experience early in life could turn a kitten from a generally sociable breed into a fraidy-cat, or one from a normally relaxed breed into a nervous Nellie. The reverse is also true: A member of a breed known as passive could turn into a real party animal in the care of people who went out of their way to give it affection, stimulation and opportunities to play.

Brief profiles of some popular breeds follow. If one of these seems like your ideal cat, learn more about it by reading, asking someone who has a member of that breed, or going to a cat show where you can see a number of them on display and talk to their breeders.

Popular Shorthairs

Abyssinian: The strong, silent type, Abys are loving, smart and devoted, like the Siamese, but without the constant chitchat. They have blue or ruddy coats with hairs that show dark and light bands.

American Shorthair: These sturdy, easygoing kitties descend from the cats that crossed the Atlantic to help establish the original U.S. and Canadian colonies. They're self-reliant but friendly.

Bombay: Bred to resemble black panthers, these sleek, glossy cats with bright copper eyes are active and curious. They're easygoing, enjoy human company, and like warm laps even more.

British Shorthair: Descended from British house and farm cats, they are large (up to 18 lbs.) and may seem aloof because they're so self-reliant. Gentle and genial, they don't like much handling.

Burmese: These descendants of Oriental temple cats are available in both the sturdy, rounded American and slender, angular European versions. Both are bright, friendly, loyal, playful and easygoing.

California Spangled: Expect to pay top dollar for these Hollywood glamour cats that have the look of cheetahs and snow leopards, but without the wild ancestors. They're gentle and sociable.

Chartreux: Since the 1700s, the Chartreux has been the national cat of France. These big, stocky kitties have high-pitched voices and sometimes chirp. They're calm and observant.

Cornish Rex: Extroverted athletes, they make high jumps their specialty. These slender cats with gracefully arched bodies, small heads and huge ears are best known for their wavy coats.

Devon Rex: "All ears" like their Cornish cousins, the Devons have rippling coats rather than wavy ones. Some breeders claim they're hypoallergenic. They're definitely bright-eyed and full of fun.

Egyptian Mau: Bred from Egyptian and Italian stock, these smart, spotted pusses with the anxious expressions can actually be quite self-reliant. They'd rather have human companions, though.

Exotic Shorthair: These "Persians in pajamas" have dense double coats, gentle dispositions and squeaky voices. Livelier and more curious than Persians, they share their distinctive facial type.

Havana Brown: Strong contenders in feline track-and-field events, these climbers, leapers and pouncers also enjoy playing hide-and-seek with their people. They're sweet-tempered and sociable.

Japanese Bobtail: Depicted in their native land as good luck symbols, these cats with rabbit-like tails have hind legs that are slightly longer than the ones in front. They're alert, loving and playful.

Korat: These muscular, rounded cats with silver-blue coats and light green eyes descend from the original house cats of Thailand. Not for the timid human, they're opinionated, pushy pussycats.

Manx: These cats of many colors are known for their short or missing tails and their hopping gait, which results from longer rear legs that elevate their rumps. They're easygoing family cats.

Ocicat: Spotted to resemble their wild cousins, Ocis are actually the tame descendants of Siamese, Abyssinians and American Shorthairs. They're playful and enjoy human company.

Russian Blue: These gentle cats take awhile to bond with their humans, becoming affectionate, loyal companions in their own good time. They have glossy, gray-blue coats and sweet expressions.

Scottish Fold: Folds are smart, devoted one-person cats with gentle features and small, round ears that cover the head like a cap.

Singapura: If you need to sneak a cat into a no-pets building, choose this pocket-size puss. Adults weigh as little as four pounds. They're quietly devoted and have beautiful eyes with natural "liner."

Sphynx: With "peach fuzz" instead of fur and often whiskerless, these wide-eyed, big-eared kitties must stay indoors to be comfortable. Their bodies feel like suede and they're full of mischief.

Tonkinese: With softly shaded markings rather than the "points" of some Oriental breeds, these aqua-eyed beauties result from Siamese-Burmese crosses. They're affectionate, bright and playful.

Popular Longhairs

American Curl: If you want a quiet, affectionate pet who doubles as a conversation piece, this plume-tailed cat, with small, rounded ears that curl toward the top of its head, fills the bill.

Angora: With athletic grace and silky coats of many colors, these cats of Turkish ancestry date from the 1400s. They look delicate but have energy to burn. They're party animals who love to show off.

Balinese: Basically a long-haired Siamese with a feathery tail, the Balinese is just as loving, vocal and demanding, but a little less athletic. This breed is also great with children.

Birman: These "sacred cats of Burma" are sweet and gentle, but make sure they get their fair share of human affection. They have striking color points, snow-white feet and big, bright blue eyes.

Himalayan: Sturdily built like Persians, but with the "points" of their Siamese ancestors (darker color on the ears, face, paws and tail), Himmies are relaxed and friendly with a touch of showmanship.

Maine Coon: Contrary to legend, these big (up to 22 lbs.), gentle darlings have no raccoon ancestors, just striking facial markings and bushy tails. They're loving family pets and do well in cold climates.

Norwegian Forest Cat: Also bred for cold weather, these fluffy, hardy cats have gorgeous, water-repellent double coats and full ruffs that resemble lions' manes. They're calm and self-contained.

Persian: The most popular longhairs, Persians are prized for their quiet, sweet temperaments and glorious coats. A word of caution however – those with extreme "pug" faces often develop eye, nose and dental problems.

Ragdoll: Born to cuddle, Ragdolls get their name from their habit of going limp when held. They're large, usually with color points, and very gentle. Lovers, not fighters, they're perfect for kids and indoor life.

Siberian: Large, sturdy and resourceful, these cats have thick coats that protected their ancestors from harsh Russian winters. Energetic and agile, Siberians are friendly, but they're not lap cats.

Somali: Like their short-haired cousins, the Abyssinians, Somalis are graceful and soft-voiced, with ticked coats. Their arched backs and tiptoe walk give them a predatory look. They're happiest outdoors.

Turkish Van: These mostly white cats sport colorful patches on their heads and tails and are enthusiastic swimmers. They're self-contained and bond gradually with people who earn their respect.

ADOPTIONS

If you're going to adopt a purebred, deal with a breeder rather than a pet store. Pet stores almost always obtain their kittens from breeders, so eliminate the middleman and go to the source, where you can find out as much as possible about your kitten-to-be. Plan to visit the cattery at least once before you choose your new family member, at least twice before you take him or her home.

Each of my cats arrived in my life in a different manner with its own set of legalities attached, so I'll use their stories to illustrate the do's and don'ts of adoptions and rescues.

The laws mentioned here apply to Florida, where we live. Since regulations vary from place to place, refer any questions to your veterinarian or one of these agencies: state department of agriculture, county animal care and control facility, municipal government or local ASPCA or Humane Society.

Cleo was raised in an indoor cattery with five littermates, a dozen other Siamese and several humans. She romped constantly with her feline family, and her breeder handled her gently and frequently from the age of one week to make sure she would socialize well with humans.

Yet Cleo, I now realize, was weaned too early. I was eager to adopt her, and the breeder, with two litters of youngsters on her hands and another on the way, was even more eager to see some of the kittens depart as soon as they reached eight weeks of age, the minimum legal age for adoptions in which money changes hands.

Even though she's now a middle-aged lady, Cleo has never outgrown her kittenish habit of kneading, although she gradually stopped suckling my neck (perhaps because she disliked the nickname Vampire Kitty) as she reached maturity. Since adopting her, I've learned that many feline behavior experts recommend allowing kittens to stay with their mothers until they're at least 12 weeks old and emotionally ready to be weaned. While I'm pleased that Cleo wants to stay so close to me, some people might prefer less of a "paws-on" relationship.

Other than that, Cleo's adoption was a good example of the right way to do things. The breeder gave me an "official certificate of veterinary inspection for small animals" from the state department of agriculture and consumer services. This document is required by law in any adoption that involves a fee. It applies equally to breeders offering $500 purebreds, individuals selling pets for $10 or $25 through the classified ads, and children enticing their neighbors with boxes of kittens of uncertain ancestry marked "$1 each."

The veterinary certificate required by law is quite detailed. It includes the name, address and phone number of both breeder and veterinarian, plus license number for the latter, dates of all shots given the kittens, type of medicine, manufacturer and lot number for each inoculation, how long each shot is effective and who administered it.

It includes the veterinarian's signed statement that says, "The above animal was examined by me on the date shown below... and, to the best of my knowledge... exhibits no signs of contagious or infectious diseases, and shows no evidence of internal or external parasites, with the possible exception of fleas and ticks. Further, to the best of my knowledge, the animal has not been exposed to rabies, nor did (it) originate from an area under a quarantine for rabies." It's a felony to falsify or alter one of these certificates.

Cleo's breeder attached her own statement that her cattery was free of feline leukemia and feline infectious peritonitis (two of the biggest killers of kittens) and provided tips on feeding, vitamin supplements and hygiene. She agreed in writing to accept the return of a kitten if a veterinarian recommended it because of a health problem that she was unaware of, provided the doctor examined the kitten within two business days. She added, "I will only sell a kitten if I feel certain that this kitten is one hundred percent healthy and lovable."

Even without such assurances, the "pet lemon law" protects people who buy cats that prove to have undisclosed ailments, helping them to arrange for an exchange,

28

refund or reimbursement of medical bills. Besides being required by law, the signed veterinary certificate is your best protection in case something goes wrong and you decide to call off the adoption.

That takes care of the legalities. On to the fun stuff.

Touring a cattery allows you to meet a whole litter of kittens, their mother and usually their father, too.

Try to arrange a time when you can meet the sire, because scientists say up to sixty percent of a kitten's personality comes from its father. If Daddy seems overly wild or withdrawn, you might want to keep searching.

Watching the kittens interact with their mother and littermates can tell you a lot, too. Ideally, Momcat will be warmly affectionate to all her babies, without playing favorites, and the kittens will chase and wrestle each other without ganging up on one individual. A kitten who experiences non-stop love from its mother and acceptance from its siblings early in life is virtually certain to become an affectionate, playful companion for you.

It's a plus if the kitten is raised "underfoot," treated like part of the breeder's family. That way, it will be used to children, adults of both sexes and maybe dogs or other species of pets. It will also have excellent mental and nervous system development because of all the sights, sounds and sensations it experiences.

Look for a cattery that's clean and tidy, but with a relaxed atmosphere so you can interact with the litter and the mother cat on at least two visits.

Cleo's breeder let me roll around on the floor with the whole bunch, observe them at mealtime and help with claw clipping. After this much socializing, you'll probably start developing a special bond with one of the kittens. Most important, you'll be able to tell if any of the kitties seem ill, cranky or lethargic – which is

29

another definite sign that you should continue shopping around.

You probably won't be able to do more than just view the father cat. As a "working" tom, he's likely to be segregated in his own kitty condo, away from the females in order to prevent unplanned pregnancies.

If you love a particular breed but feel you can't afford a kitten, you might still be able to obtain a wonderful example of the breed. All you need is patience and the willingness to accept a full-grown cat. Perfectly healthy, beautiful purebreds only one to two years old are sometimes offered at little or no charge simply because they no longer compete in shows or meet the needs of a cattery's breeding program. (A cattery, like any business, must make room for the moneymakers.) Check the classified ads or ask around at cat shows.

Free felines are not covered by the laws that regulate sales, so demand assurances of health and disposition in writing, and make it a condition of adoption that you be allowed to have the cat examined by your vet and returned if he or she finds anything wrong. A breeder eager to find a loving home for a surplus kitty should readily agree.

RESCUES

While Cleo's adoption was by the book and trouble-free, Hope's was a rescue fraught with red tape and a swamp of nasty legalities I was lucky to sidestep.

Several summers ago, I started feeding Pandora, a feral Siamese, on my patio. On the following October 4th, she presented me with three adorable kittens who, thanks to good timing and foster parenting by my kindhearted veterinarian, all found great homes in time for the holidays. I would gladly have rounded up Pandora to be spayed and vaccinated, but this wily kitty was impossible to catch. The following spring she brought me three more beautiful babies who joined her for feedings.

One evening a few months later, my neighbor (I'll call him Joe) came home late and stumbled over one of the kitties in the dark. He playfully reached for her, and she bit his finger.

When I heard about this a few days later, I understood why one of the kittens hadn't been showing up for dinner. Joe was worried about rabies, and the vet who cared for his cats told Joe to catch the kitten and place her under quarantine so he could avoid painful rabies shots. After a few days at a local shelter, the kitten was returned to Joe and his wife (call her Jane), who promised to keep her under observation for 10 days, caged and away from their other pets.

One day, I stopped by to visit the little one and found what looked like a very sick kitty hiding in the back of a large crate on the neighbors' porch. She had plenty of room, food and water and a clean litter tray, but seemed fearful and feverish and had the sniffles. Doing without air conditioning in the middle of a July heat wave couldn't have been much fun for her, either. I wanted to intervene, but, trying not to be a nosy neighbor, I left, promising to visit again soon.

I didn't get the chance. A couple of days later, Jane was at my door in tears, saying the kitten was about to be killed. The vet who had originally ordered the quarantine (let's call him Dr. No) had somehow convinced the county authorities that this sick, defenseless ten-week-old ball of fluff was a dangerous feral who might be rabid and couldn't be trusted not to bite again.

Saying he "wouldn't even touch her to put her down,"

Dr. No ordered one of his flunkies to transport the kitten from Joe's and Jane's place to the county animal control shelter. Since the test for rabies requires analysis of brain tissue that can only be obtained after death, the kitten was now on the feline equivalent of Death Row.

I told Jane to call the shelter and, if the kitten was still alive, ask that she be given a stay of execution until we could get there. It turned out that our kitty, next in line for euthanasia, had escaped the needle by minutes. Fortunately, shelter personnel were willing to give us a chance to straighten out the mess in person.

The pussycat posse piled in my car and headed for the shelter, where we did our best to convince the woman in charge that Dr. No had made a dreadful mistake. I called my veterinarian, Dr. Andrew Faigen of For Cats Only in West Palm Beach, Florida (He's a good guy, so we'll use his real name), and explained the situation. He agreed to examine the kitten, and everyone else agreed to abide by his decision – to treat her if she had a good chance of growing up to enjoy life, or euthanize her if she was too sick to save.

After examining the pitiful, emaciated kitty, who'd been getting sicker and sicker as she was shuttled from one place to another, Dr. Faigen diagnosed her illness as a virus that was causing serious respiratory problems. It would take a lengthy hospital stay, intravenous feeding and medication to give her a good shot at recovery, and even then we might lose her.

But, he said, "There's hope."

I said, "Then that's her name" and asked him to start treating Hope immediately.

As soon as Hope was able to eat on her own, I began making lunchtime visits to the cat hospital to tempt her taste buds with roast turkey, poached salmon and such. After about a week, Dr. Faigen and I were rewarded with our first purrs of thanks. I don't think Hope has stopped purring since.

A few days and $900 later, I brought home a skinny but happy kitten who was well on the way to recovery. I know I'll never lose Hope because, safe inside a loving home, she shows no interest in the world beyond the front door.

I officially adopted Hope when I started paying her medical bills, but (something I didn't know until months later) she would have been legally mine anyway, because the law says ferals belong to whoever is feeding them. As it turned out, Joe caught nothing but a good scare from Hope's bite ("For goodness sake," says Hope, "I was only protecting myself from a strange human who lunged for me!"), but if he had contracted rabies and wanted someone to sue, I would have been the perfect target.

Dr. No, who evidently knew little about cats and cared even less, made a bad situation worse. Without his intervention, Hope would have completed her quarantine with my neighbors and I could have then taken her to Dr. Faigen before she made the critical list. For some reason we can only guess at, Dr. No mistook the gleam in Hope's eyes – perhaps a sign of superior intelligence – for rabies or evil intent. We'll never know why he decided to cut the quarantine short, or why county officials let him.

Almost losing Hope taught me another valuable lesson: All veterinarians are not created equal. Some treat dogs almost exclusively and are wary of cats, or even actively dislike them. A cats-only practice like Dr. Faigen's has a lot to recommend it. He's one of a growing number of veterinary specialists who understand felines' special needs and, just as important, chose this speciality because they, too, are bonafide cat lovers.

While all this was going on, I continued to feed Pandora and Hope's siblings, who I named Faith and Charity. Faith earned her name by adopting me and camping on my patio, convinced I'd let her inside one day if she refused to give up. Charity, a frisky black and white youngster who visited less frequently, began showing signs of becoming a teenage tomcat, and was promptly renamed Charlie.

Between work and giving Hope the round-the-clock care she still needed, I didn't see how I could adopt any more kitties, and my wallet agreed. Fortunately, the fates stepped in and worked everything out.

Pandora showed up with a new litter of kittens, three midnight black ones this time. As she brought me these new mouths to feed, I could almost hear her asking, "Why didn't anyone tell me about birth control?" As I stocked up on Meow Mix, turkey and catnip, I wondered the same thing.

Over the next week, Faith really settled in, leaving her cardboard cat house on my patio only when nature called or she felt the urge to chase a lizard. Charlie, whose visits were now few and far between, seemed to have his paws full helping Pandora with the new kittens.

Soon Hope got better and I got richer. Pandora, Charlie and the kids moved a block away, where someone desperately in need of cats took them all in. (Charlie came back once to tell me about it.) Faith hung in there, purring in my lap when I went out to feed her and pleading with Hope whenever she appeared in the window.

Faith needn't have begged because she'd had me

wrapped me around her little paw for months. I took her to Dr. Faigen, who gave her all the necessary shots, flushed out her ears to get rid of mites, had her bathed to eliminate fleas, and pronounced her in perfect health. Rescue No. 2 was complete, and like Hope, Faith became a house cat and never looked back.

When someone tells you feral cats are impossible to tame, laugh loudly and refer them to my girls, who will set them straight.

Even people who encourage the adoption of ferals often say you can't socialize a half-wild kitten that's more than two months old. I even saw an article to this effect in a national cat magazine just a few months ago. Whoever circulates these rumors must never have dealt with kittens like Faith, Hope, Charlie and the litter that came before them. Except for Hope, all these kittens moved into their permanent homes when they were adolescents. Faith was eight months old when she finally crossed the threshold.

Making friends with a feral is a gradual process requiring months of consistent feeding, soft words and gentle gestures, but there's no statute of limitations on the wonders love can work.

In any litter of ferals, the kittens can vary greatly in their response to people. Nature generally makes one kitten sociable, one wary and the others somewhere in between. When I first got to know them (at about six weeks of age), Hope was fearlessly affectionate, Faith was friendly but reserved, and Charlie was skittish, although grateful for the handouts.

Hope's bad experience could have turned her against people forever, but, except for the days when she was sickest, she's been a cuddlepuss all along. Faith needed a long time to overcome her shyness, but now she's just as affectionate as Hope. I can't say for sure how Charlie turned out, but it's been two years since he and Pandora came to visit, so I feel certain all's well. The neighborhood has been free of homeless kittens, which must mean Pandora's new human has had her spayed (Hallelujah!).

Shelter Kitties

Like rescued ferals, felines adopted from shelters seem to sense they've been granted a new lease on life, and most spend the rest of their days repaying the favor with affection and good behavior. Dealing with a shelter, you might be able to acquire a wonderful companion at a bargain price.

There are exceptions, though. Since there's little opportunity to get to know a prospective pet at a shelter, and very few allow cats to be taken home for a trial period, you're usually left with more questions than answers.

Shelter personnel can tell you only as much as they know. The only shelter kitties that come with information on age, health and ancestry are those that were dropped off by people no longer able to keep them. Others are brought in by people who found them wandering near their homes, or as the result of animal control roundups. In these cases, the information you see posted on the cats' cages can only represent the best guesses of the shelter staff and its overworked veterinarian.

We'd never want to discourage a good deed, but if you obtain a cat from a shelter, be aware that it could have health or behavioral problems that become apparent only after you've taken it home and fallen in love. Shelters are generally exempt from the "pet lemon laws" that protect people who adopt cats from pet stores or breeders.

Before you adopt, get all aspects of the agreement in

writing – those that spell out your recourse as a consumer in case of trouble as well as your responsibility to the cat and the shelter.

Cat Shows

Cat shows can be great places to spot a kitten you'd like to adopt, or at least meet members of his or her immediate family, but it's not the place to formalize an adoption. The breeder is probably busy showing several felines and may be trying to make a sale or arrange a mating on the side (for a cat, that is).

When you notice a potential pet at a show, introduce yourself to the breeder, ask a few simple questions about the breed, the kitten, whether it's available and if so, at what price. Then ask for the breeder's business card and agree on a day when you can telephone for more information. Only after an opportunity to have all your questions answered, on a day when the breeder is much less harried, will you know enough to decide whether you want to schedule a visit to the cattery.

Cleo adds this pussyfootnote: "Say what you will, when a cat decides to adopt you, you're adopted. The many ways in which it happens only go to show what *purr*-suasive, *purr*-sistent beasties we are."

On the Way Home

However your new cat comes into your life, the final step in the adoption should be a stop at the veterinarian's office to get acquainted, have an initial checkup and receive whatever inoculations are needed.

If you're not happy with the reception you and your

kitty receive from the first doctor, try another, and a third if necessary. For your cat's health and your peace of mind, it's important to develop a good, friendly relationship with a veterinarian whose medical training is matched by a sincere concern for the patient. During the first visit, watch how the doctor interacts with your cat. Then ask what you should do in case of emergency. If he or she tells you anything less than, "Call me anytime, day or night, whenever you think you need to," you still haven't found the right one for your kitty.

Finally, look for a veterinarian who keeps up with the latest developments in cat care and treatment. Most of the diagnostic tools and surgical techniques that are available in human medicine are also available for cats, but all vets may not be aware of them.

While we were writing this, a routine blood test revealed that Cleo had elevated liver enzymes. Dr. Faigen X-rayed her, discovered she also had a liver that was much smaller than usual, and recommended a sonogram to rule out any disease or structural defect. I knew about using ultrasound to monitor babies in the womb, but had no idea it was also being used for cats.

Fortunately, Cleo's little liver received the all-clear, but if she had been developing a disease, the sonogram would have allowed us to treat it in its earliest stages when chances of recovery are greatest.

CREATING A CAT-FRIENDLY ENVIRONMENT

Whatever type of cat you choose, the basics for a happy home life are the same: good food, pleasant living conditions and friendly relations with other members of the household. Cats see things a bit differently than the rest of us, though. To obtain the unique feline perspective, I'm turning this chapter over to the experts – and you'll get it straight from the cat's mouth.

🐾   🐾   🐾

What Cats Need Out of Life

By HOPE SMITHER

ALL a cat needs to be healthy is cat food and water. But most people define cat food far too narrowly. Sure, we kitties like beef, poultry and seafood along with our kibble, but some of us also like salad, pasta, fruit and ice cream.

Cats who are "the only child" may want to observe the same mealtimes as their adoptive parents, but in a multi-cat household like ours, it makes sense to leave bowls of dry food and water out all the time so each of us can nibble when we like.

We'll take care of emptying the food bowls, but you'll

need to freshen our water at least three times a day. We have special taste buds that allow us to savor water's flavor, and when it doesn't taste fresh enough, we start seeking alternate sources, like a dripping faucet, a garden hose, or even (if we have to!) a toilet bowl.

Brands marked "complete nutrition for all stages of a cat's life" meet the needs of most felines from recently weaned kittens to nursing Momcats. Those marked "100 percent nutritionally complete for adult cats" are fine for kitties past their first birthdays who have no special needs. In order to use these labels, foods must go through rigorous analysis, first by human scientists, then in feeding trials with the real experts – hundreds of hungry cats with high standards, like me.

Finding a food that pleases all your felines is a little harder than simply identifying one that's healthful, but it shouldn't take too long. We kitties, like the curmudgeons who review restaurants, are emphatic in giving our opinions.

If your cat chows down enthusiastically, then comes back for more a few hours later, all's well. If, instead, your puss swats bits of cereal out of the bowl and uses them as hockey pucks, turns the bowl over on the floor, or (this is Faith's favorite trick) wraps it in paper napkins to signal that it's ready for the trash, you need to find another brand.

Some humans think that if they love us, they must show it by buying the most expensive cat food available. That's really not necessary. We'd rather you fed us a nice, affordable brand for regular meals – our favorites are Meow Mix and Friskies' Dental Diet – and saved the rest of your money for treats and catnip. (Mom recently offered us some ritzy $2.50-a-pound lamb-and-rice formula some human recommended, and I'm afraid our response wasn't very nice. After a single sniff, we all turned our backs on the stuff and started making noises like we were hawking up five-pound furballs.)

Enough about the basics. What a kitty gourmet really lives for is snacks. And prowling for them gives us a healthy outlet for our predatory instincts as well as an opportunity to indulge our individual tastes. When it comes to treats, each of us has a distinctive style.

When I first came here, I was a skinny young kitten recovering from a serious illness, and Mom did everything she could to tempt my palate. She let me sit on the dining room table and taste each item on her plate. I learned that turkey, chicken, fish and shrimp are delicious, long noodles are great for tug-of-war, canned fruit is slippery and fresh veggies are crunchy. I developed a taste for a wide range of foods, from chicken soup to garden salads made of lettuce, tomatoes, celery and such.

Now that I'm three years old and weigh twelve pounds, my "feed the starving kitten" routine doesn't work as well as it used to, but that's okay, since I don't seem to have a kitten's metabolism anymore. When Mom's eating, I content myself with sitting patiently on the floor, my soulful gaze the only reminder that I'd appreciate a bite. That is, unless there's shrimp, salmon, tomatoes or peaches on the menu. Then I jump on the table and stick my nose in the plate. At that point, Mom usually gives in and shares.

Faith used to be shy and retiring, but for the past year or so, she's had no problem speaking up when she smells something she'd like to taste. Her favorite treats are canned tuna (especially the juice), roast turkey and broiled swordfish.

Cleo, being Siamese, has an advantage over the rest of us when it comes to begging. She just crosses her eyes and gives one of those "silent meows" that are impossible to resist. Fortunately, the only treats she's passionate about are fruit and yogurt.

By the way, doctors say there are three foods you should never give a kitty: pork, onions and chocolate. I don't mind – in fact, that doesn't sound like a combination any self-respecting feline gourmet would ever WANT to eat.

Here are some recipes from my fantasy cookbook, "Meowvelous Meals."

BREAKFAST IN BED

1 pot of coffee, ready to brew
2 waffles
1 bottle maple-flavored syrup
1 sleepy human

Hop on the kitchen counter to press the "start" button on the coffeemaker. Wait until the pot is almost full, then wake your human by meowing plaintively until she comes to see what's wrong. Paw at the toaster until she gets the idea and inserts the waffles. Then go back to bed to keep the sheets warm. When your human shows up with toasted waffles and syrup, be nice. Move over and let her have some of the bed, and she'll probably let you have some waffle.

SHRIMPLY DELICIOUS

½ lb fresh shrimp
½ cup minced celery
2 Tbs mayonnaise

3 Tbs chili sauce
Romaine leaves for garnish

Have your human shell, devein, boil and chill the shrimp, then chop them and mix with me-ownaise, chili sauce and celery. Use your claws to shred romaine on a plate, then have your human pour the mixture over it. Use your paws to locate shrimp. Eat your fill, then flick the rest to the other cats. Leave the salad for your human.

TUNA CATSERROLE

6 oz noodles, boiled al dente
6-oz can white tuna (dolphin-safe, please)
1 small can evaporated milk, diluted with a little water
½ cup fresh mushrooms, finely chopped and sautéed
½ cup chopped green beans, fresh or frozen
Salt, pepper, garlic powder
Crushed potato chips, crackers or bread crumbs for
  topping

Have your human chop and sauté the mush-rooms, chop the green beans, and boil and drain the noodles. Then ask him to combine the tuna, milk, mushrooms and beans in an oven-safe fry-ing pan, and simmer gently until the flavors mingle. Have him add the noodles, stir until they're nicely coated with sauce, season with salt, pep-per and garlic powder, sprinkle with your choice of topping, and bake at 375° for 30 minutes.

Doing all this properly requires a lot of work on your human's part, so invite him to join you for dinner.

THANKSGIVING BEAST FEAST

1 turkey, seasoned with garlic and roasted with
  pan gravy
1 can cranberry sauce
Gobs of mashed potatoes made with butter
  and cream

Recruit a human to roast the turkey and re-
move it from the oven, open the cranberry sauce,
peel, boil and drain the potatoes and add the
butter and cream. Offer helping paws when it's
time to mash.

Serve with a flourish to as many kitties as
you can fit at the table. All other Thanksgiving
dishes, no matter how traditional, are a waste of
time and effort. If it won't impress a cat, why
bother to make it?

FRUIT PURR-FAIT

1 scoop vanilla frozen yogurt
¼ cup finely chopped fresh peaches or strawberries

It's best if your human prepares this, since
you could freeze your paws off messing with the
frozen yogurt carton. Ask her to layer the yogurt and fruit in a pretty dish that's shallow
enough to accommodate your whiskers.

The Scoop on Kitty Litter

By FAITH SMITHER

CATS vary in their preferences about litter box design and type of litter, but all require a reasonable amount of privacy and sanitary conditions resembling those of the best operating rooms.

You've heard about the rich lady who sold her Rolls because the ashtray was dirty? Well, that's how I feel about my commode. Whatever I step on in there had better be scrupulously clean and feel right under my paws, or I'll stamp my feet in annoyance until Mom makes it fresh again.

I may be prissier than the average puss, but most cats say they want their boxes cleaned at least once a day, and twice is better.

As for the box itself, it should be a little bigger than the cat who will use it, shaped so he or she can turn around comfortably, and high enough on the sides so aiming won't be a problem. It should be in an out-of-the-way place that's not too close to the feeding area. The color doesn't matter, as long as it won't clash outrageously with the decor. Some cats like hooded boxes, while others prefer open ones hidden behind curtains or screens.

The ideal home will have one box per cat, plus one for emergencies. Since we live in an apartment, we made do for a long time with two boxes, one in each bathroom. After I presented her with a petition signed by all three of us, though, Mom added a third box in the master bath. I'm now lobbying for a whole powder room of my own, but she says that's out of the question.

Kitty litter is crucial. There are dozens of brands made of everything from clay to wood shavings to lemon-scented newspaper pellets. (The last one doesn't make any sense to me, since citrus is a well-known cat repellent. If you try this type, get the unscented variety.)

Since our ancestors' original litter was desert sand, many of us prefer the newer, scoopable litters that are sandy in texture. These are especially good at absorbing urine. The litter clumps, keeping moisture away from the kitty until the housekeeper can clean the box.

If you live with more than one cat, consider using two or more different types of litter so everyone can choose his or her favorite. Both humans and felines prefer the low-tracking brands. (We like Tidy Cats' multi-cat formula and Ever Fresh clumping litter.) For the humans, less litter tracked through the house means less time cleaning floors. This also pleases the pusses in residence, since the less we have to deal with those indoor predators, vacuum cleaners, the better.

Plastic liners for litter boxes are optional as far as we kitties are concerned, but most humans like them because they make cleanup easier. What's important is that the litter be changed at least once a week and the boxes washed with mild soap and water as often as necessary to keep them immaculate. If persistent odor is a problem, the restroom attendant can add a little bleach to the soap and water solution or spray the boxes with Lysol before they're refilled.

The only time NOT to clean out the litter box is when you're relocating. That's when people should take along a box containing slightly soiled litter to let their cats know they have a new home.

These days, we're all encouraged to "think outside the box," but messing outside the box is another matter, distressing to cats and humans alike. When this happens, it's a cry for help, an otherwise tidy feline's last resort to communicate that the box has an unpleasant smell or the litter is the wrong texture.

If these matters are attended to and the situation still doesn't improve, please don't blame the kitty. Just make an appointment with the doctor to find out what's wrong. I've met dirty dogs and dirty birds, but believe me, there's no such thing as a dirty cat.

❖ ❖ ❖

Cleo Decorates from Scratch

By CLEO SMITHER

INTERIOR design is highly subjective, but like my heroine, Martha Stewart, I know the good things when I see them. Here's my short course in decorating with kitty comforts in mind.

We cats are sensitive to touch, so textures are very important to us – the softer and silkier, the better. Colors don't matter as much, since we don't distinguish them as well as humans do. Given a choice, we'd prefer the violets, blues and greens at the cool end of the spectrum, which is most visible to us.

When furnishing for felines, keep our daily activities in mind. For most of us past the first blush of kittenhood, this means 'round-the-clock catnaps punctuated by meals, playtime and periods of deep sleep.

The bed is the focal point of feline decor, and it should be as big and luxurious as possible, with linens soft enough to nestle in and a mattress firm enough to double as a trampoline. A queen-size pillowtop mattress with a comforter for burrowing is great for catnaps and games of hide-and-seek. We got one of these last year and we all love it.

When the time comes for serious sleeping, the best spot is in the exact center of the bed, on a human pillow. Most people are willing to act as kitty cushions, especially if the cat in question is as adorable as I am. The hard part is keeping them still. Kitties take note: Bedding down behind your human's knees is safest because you'll have something to cling to when the tossing and turning begins.

While the bed is our perennial favorite, we also need a variety of napping spots. Discovering new ones is a popular form of feline entertainment, so give your kitties lots of choices. Mom followed my advice and did a pretty good job. A survey of our apartment reveals 35 nifty napping nooks, and that's a conservative estimate.

First and best, there's my round, pink, fuzzy bed under Mom's desk. It's lined with a purple velvet cushion and I love to lie there when she's working. (She says I inspire her.) Next, for short naps only, there's the computer monitor. When Mom replaced the old one recently, she bought a large, sturdy model with a spacious surface area so Hope, the nerd, could recline there comfortably. Another neat feature of Mom's office is her four bookcases. I'm counting them as only four napping spots, but they actually have as many possibilities as there are shelves.

In the living room, there's a huge cat tree with four carpeted trays for napping or surveying our kingdom. We also have a roomy sofa, two hideouts in the end tables that double as cabinets, two easy chairs with napping nooks under them, four dining chairs, and a tent under the dining room table, which is draped with a long cloth so we can pretend we're camping out.

On the floor of the hall closet (where we're usually not allowed), there's a cat carrier lined with a sheet; it makes a nice place to get away from it all on stressful days.

The bedroom is filled with places to nap: a cushioned Windsor chair with some of my favorite stuffed animals, a big lounge chair and ottoman that hold several more, a picnic basket lined with soft old curtains (Faith's favorite hideaway), a small cat tree with one napping tray, and a carpeted tower with three cubbyholes as well as napping space on the top. For those Prozac moments, there's that reliable refuge – under the bed.

In the clothes closet, there's a laundry basket full of sweaters topped with a fluffy rug, and the master bath has a towel rack that's super for snoozing. Finally, there's a table on our screened balcony that's positioned just right for basking in the sun.

Even the most dedicated cat can't nap all the time. Eventually we must wake, stretch and scratch, so the wise human will designate several areas where we can rake our claws to our hearts' content. First, install a large cat tree made of real logs in a prominent place where we can carve our special territorial hieroglyphics for all to see. This should do fine for vertical clawing. Sometimes we also like to exercise our claws horizontally, so offer your fur persons a carpeted scratching pad in another prominent place.

If these special scratching places feel good to us, we should have no reason to use your furniture. Still, a word about upholstery is in order. Some cats, especially we Siamese, have a thing about wool, which we find almost as delightful as catnip. Expecting us to leave a wool rug alone is just too much to ask. All cats love to scratch fabrics with vertical weaves, so raw silk and corduroy are very hard to resist. Denim, canvas, tapestry and cut velvet, on the other paw, are either unpleasant to the touch or hard on the claws, so you can count on us to leave those alone.

If you love your cats, potted plants and cut flowers are best left out of your decorating scheme, since many are poisonous or at least toxic enough to cause an upset tummy. If you must have some greenery around, ask your veterinarian for a list of plants that are relatively safe.

Of the holiday varieties, poinsettia usually just makes us gag, but mistletoe can cause serious harm. Christmas trees present an array of dangers, from prickly pine needles to tempting glass ornaments and strings of lights. And if an adventurous feline decides to climb the tree for a closer look at the angel on top, the whole thing can come crashing down, causing enough of a ruckus to make even Santa Claus grumpy.

Fortunately, there are plenty of alternatives to live plants, like silk trees, and bouquets and wreaths of dried flowers. Last year we even found a catproof Christmas tree. A lovely arrangement of dried plant and flower materials, it's complete with little white lights and designed to hang on the wall where it's safe from inquiring paws.

Toys and Games: A Cat Panel Tells It Like It Is!

CLEO: Give me a catnip toy and a safe place to sleep off the effects and I'm happy. Mom says it's OK if I get a little giddy, as long as I promise not to drive.

FAITH: Catnip is OK, but what I really love is chasing Mr. Bat as Mom makes him fly overhead, or pouncing on the fake snake she calls the Cat Charmer.

HOPE: That's fun, but I like to sit on the computer and play cat and mouse. I also get a kick out of chasing balls, especially when Mom takes turns fetching. Catching fly balls that bounce off the ceiling is cool, too, and lately I've been learning to grab them with my paws.

CLEO: With our boundless curiosity, we don't even need toys to amuse ourselves. There are rolls of toilet tissue to shred anytime, and paper bags to explore whenever the groceries come. Every so often, a cardboard box arrives at the front door, filled with tissue paper that's wonderful to nestle in – although I have to wait for Mom to pull out whatever else is in there before it becomes a suitable plaything. Then there are my games of tag. All I need are a couple of subordinate cats to chase.

HOPE: Good luck finding some. How about Kitty Lump and Mole, the games I invented to play in bed? When you're under the covers, you're the Kitty Lump and everybody else gets to pounce on you. When you're on top, Mom puts her arm under the covers and makes it burrow like a Mole to give you predator practice.

FAITH: Some predator you are. I go right for the biggest prize, Mom's bare foot. The only problem is, sometimes after I've "killed" it, she sneaks up on me and clips my claws.

HOPE: Why do you think I spend so much time under the covers?

CAT TALK!

It takes a perceptive human to understand what a "fur person" is saying because cats express themselves with everything from their eyes, ears and whiskers to swipes of their paws and twitches of their tails – in addition to a wide range of meows, chirps, catcalls and purrs.

Cats are definitely a breed apart, and trying too hard to think like one will only leave a poor human with furrowed brow and twisted brain. To connect with your kitty, just be receptive to his or her signals and learn to reply in a way that a feline can appreciate. Even if you're not always completely sure what either of you is saying, you'll strengthen your bond while enjoying each other's company.

I approach each of my cats differently, depending on her distinctive personality and the parts of my personality that it calls to.

For example, Cleo loves extended conversations, so we meow back and forth as long as she wants to chat. (People who consider this weird may stay away – or endure my comments on *their* private behavior.) At bedtime, when Cleo turns kittenish and needs to be cradled, I welcome her with open arms. After all, a cat's human companion serves as surrogate mother, and a Momcat will never push her kitten away.

Cats receive others' thoughts as images, and since Cleo reads my mind very well, I do my best to send her detailed thought pictures whenever I want her to understand something important, like a coming change in the household or the need to be boarded overnight. The tough part is remembering *not* to send pictures when it's time for something horrid, like claw clipping or flea repellent.

Connecting with Hope is much simpler. All it takes is love, love, love, food, food, food, and a willingness to share whatever's of interest on a given day, from the morning waffle to the evening news. Although Hope chirps and sings her greetings, purrs like an idling motorcycle, and expresses herself with every inch of her fluffy body, she seldom produces anything resembling a meow.

Although emotionally easygoing, Hope can be intellectually demanding. This brainy kitty enjoys challenges such as trying to catch icons on the computer screen, figuring out exactly which part of the stereo the music comes from and learning to "talk" on the phone. I try to offer enough toys and games to keep her from becoming bored.

For the first two years, communicating with timid Faith was mostly a matter of giving her space and being patient. I had to resist the urge to offer unwanted attention and simply try to provide a secure, accepting atmosphere that would allow her to feel free to approach me on her own terms, in her own good time.

Unable to explain why it was taking so long for her to become a full-fledged, indoor member of the family, Faith at first spent much of her time under the bed and was careful to stay far away from doors and windows. It was as if she feared being pitched out by anyone who thought she was in the way. It took several months for her to feel comfortable enough to sleep in bed with the rest of us or accept a snack from my hand. It was more than a year before she felt confident enough to approach me with purrs and meows and ask for attention.

Since Faith obviously felt like low cat on the totem pole, I went out of my way to bolster her self-esteem without threatening her fragile sense of security. I encouraged her to claim a high windowsill – the one with the best view – as her territory, and to fight to win whenever Hope started an impromptu wrestling match. I praised her whenever she dared to perch on the top tray of the cat tree or compete with the others to "kill" make-believe prey.

A content and confident three-year-old, Faith no longer hesitates to speak her mind with a meow, a chirp, a purr or a paw. She finally believes she doesn't have to take a back seat to anyone (no matter what Cleo says).

HOW TO SPEAK CAT (A HEAD-TO-TOE GUIDE)

❧ ❧ Vocalizing ❧ ❧

Scientists say domestic cats make more than 20 distinctive sounds, divided into three main groups: murmurs, meows and catcalls.

Murmurs include chirps of greeting, which, especially in kittens, sound remarkably like those of birds, and trills that sound like the feline version of whistling a happy tune.

The best-known murmur is the purr, which seems to relax both the cat and the person it's directed to. We know that cats purr when they're happy, and also to calm themselves in stressful situations. What no one has yet figured out is exactly where the purr originates or what biological process makes it happen. As Cleo says, "We have many mysteries, if you please." Hope is more philosophical: "I purr, therefore I am."

Meows, also called vowels, range from tiny meows to the sound of a Siamese singing for her supper, which puts most opera stars to shame.

The meow contains two distinct sounds: the "me" with which a cat greets a human or feline family member, and the "ow" that varies in intensity depending on what the cat wants. When urgently demanding something, a cat will often merge these into one insistent syllable. For example, "Mow!" means "I want my dinner" and "Now!" leaves no doubt as to the meal's timing. These might be followed by a "Wow!" demanding seconds of something that's especially delicious.

Then there are the "silent meows," which strike humans as plaintive pleas but are really just vocals outside our range of hearing.

Cats also meow to show affection, sometimes varying the sounds until they resemble human speech. For several years now, Cleo has made the effort to say "luv yoo" when she's feeling especially affectionate, and one day a few months ago, shy Faith bowled me over when she said the same thing.

Vowels also enter into house cats' vast repertoire of night sounds, which are not to be confused with the calls that wild felines make outside.

If Faith spies a stray cat from her window, she'll warn the interloper off with a series of loud, guttural meows that sound much too hellish to come from such an angelic-looking kitty.

Hope, who refuses to concern herself with territorial

disputes, sometimes sits in the hallway and sings her original songs – combinations of trills and vowels that rise and fall like someone practicing scales – purely for entertainment.

Cleo often engages in meow-a-thons that go on half an hour or more, as if she's trying to find out how long she can sing without running out of fuel.

Catcalls are the sounds a cat in the wild, or one doing the "wild thing" in mating season. They're used almost exclusively to talk to other felines. These include hisses of warning, growls of displeasure, shrieks of pain and battle cries so piercing that you'd swear a gang of banshees had invaded the neighborhood.

❧ ❧ Heads Up! ❧ ❧

Every part of a cat's head has something to say.

Vocalizing is an obvious sign that a cat has something to tell you, but a feline mouth can also smile sweetly in contentment or yawn to indicate relaxation or dispel tension.

Eyes speak volumes. A cat who wants something can often persuade you to do his bidding simply by staring at you boldly, in a way that makes you search your teeth for spinach or look down to make sure your zipper's zipped. Once you rule out these possibilities, you begin to realize there's something wrong in the cat's world, like an empty food bowl an hour past dinner time. When a cat squeezes its eyes while looking straight at you, it's a sign of deep affection that you should try to reciprocate.

By the way, cats can't really see in the dark, but they only need one-sixth the light we humans do to see well.

Their inability to see colors is another old wives' tale. The best-documented scientific tests indicate that cats can see the colors at the cool end of the spectrum, such as violet, blue and green. They can distinguish yellow, but not red. Recently I read another supposedly scientific report that said cats can see red, but not other colors. I think the scientists need to spend more time in the laboratory with their feline subjects.

The kitties I've lived with over the years seem to have had favorite colors, much the same as humans do. I can think of one in particular who loved his red toys best. Cleo is partial to purple – she says it's because she's royal.

Ears can perk up and move forward to indicate alertness, be held up and out in aggression, rotate to capture unexpected sounds or lie flat against the head to convey fear or defensiveness. If a cat has tufts at the top of its ears, it's not a sign of lynx blood, just another hearing aid. The tufts are said to enhance signals of threat and submission from other cats. If this is true, it may explain why Hope, the only one of my three with tufted ear tips, always seems to sense when one of the other cats is feeling aggressive or vulnerable.

You can tell a lot about a cat's health and mood by the way it holds its whiskers. When they're erect, held straight out and slightly upward, the cat is feeling fine and ready for anything. When they're plastered flat against the sides of the face, it's feeling threatened. When they droop, the cat may be worried or a bit under the weather.

The top and bottom rows of a cat's whiskers move independently, helping cats use them as wind detectors and as aids in locating the sources of odors. They're also part of the early warning system that allows cats to sense changes in the atmosphere that mean a storm or earthquake is on the way. Some say the span of a feline's whiskers corresponds to its girth, letting it know how wide an opening has to be in order for it to pass through comfortably.

When a cat rubs the side of its face against an object, it's marking its territory with a special scent from glands located there. When your pet puss rubs up against your ankles in similar fashion, she's claiming you as her own special person.

❧ ❧ Body Language ❧ ❧

Curled up and purring, or arching its back and spitting, a cat leaves little doubt as to its mood. Some postures in-between require explanation, though.

When a cat crouches low, it's deferring to another cat but it also indicates that it's ready to defend itself if necessary.

Lying on the back and exposing the belly is another submissive feline posture. Directed toward a human, it's a gesture of complete trust – and a request for a tummy rub.

A cat that's ready to fight lets its foe know it's on the offensive by staring with constricted pupils, head and whiskers tilted forward, claws flexed and every muscle poised to pounce.

A cat that dashes around with a bottlebrush tail and every hair standing on end has just been spooked by a person or another animal that has crossed its path unexpectedly.

Grooming is an important activity that can occupy up to a third of a cat's waking hours. It's also used as a cover for embarrassment when a kitty humiliates herself by, say, leaping to a high shelf and missing the mark.

Scratching serves two purposes: manicuring the claws and leaving a visible territorial marker. That's why a cat tree or scratching post should be displayed as prominently as possible in a room.

Kneading a favorite human, sometimes while sucking his or her skin or clothing, is a return to the warmth and security of kittenhood. When your cat does this, it's a strong pledge of allegiance and a great compliment to you. When you've had enough of this flattery, simply distract your puss by hugging her, petting her or scratching behind her ears.

The tail is one of the cat's most graceful communication tools. Carried upright, it's a friendly greeting. Wagging gently, it's a puppy-like indication of happiness. Twitching from side to side, with flicking tip, it's an invitation to play. Lashing back and forth quickly and forcefully, it warns, "Don't mess with me."

❖ ❖ Purr-Actical Applications ❖ ❖ (Advice from the Experts)

CLEO: If you're going to live with a human, you must use all your sophisticated communication techniques to wrap her around your little paw. As soon as possible, make it clear that you rule the household and will not be ignored. Then issue reminders as frequently as necessary.

Each day begins with waking your human so she (or he) can feed you, cuddle you, groom you, clean your litter box or simply amuse you. Start by stationing yourself near the bed and meowing loudly every few seconds. If there's no response after about five minutes of this, jump on the bed and purr loudly while walking on your human's tummy. If she still doesn't respond, meow even louder while walking on her head. A combination of these techniques usually works for me. Some cats add their own individual touches, like the nose bite or the eyelid tap.

Once your human is up and moving, it's your duty to involve yourself in every aspect of her day (except when you feel the need to nap). Stick your nose in her breakfast even if you don't really want anything. Watch closely while she bathes, dresses and grooms herself, making comments about her makeup and outfit. Indicate approval of the shoes she chooses by rubbing your head against them and sticking your nose in them as she tries to put them on.

Find ways to join your human in everything she does (unless it's something distasteful like cleaning la toilette). When she's writing, walk across the computer keyboard to show her you're ready to edit. When she's on the phone, interject a few meows to keep the conversation going. When she's cooking, supervise and offer to taste. When she brings in fresh, warm laundry, roll on it, then help her make the bed.

When she's reading, sit on the book to mark her place or swat something more interesting out of the bookcase. When she's watching TV, give her a kiss and look at her adoringly to remind her you're more entertaining than anything on the screen. When you want some scratching, rub your ear against her hand. When you want your throat stroked, sit beside her and stare at the ceiling. When it's time for bed, snuggle.

If the other cats in the household try to get between you and your human, glare at them, then hiss, and if they still don't get the idea, bop them on the head with your paw.

When company comes, you must walk the fine line between obvious rudeness and actually making the intruders feel welcome. Sniff the guests' feet, but don't rub up against them. Jump on their laps, but don't stay to be petted. Stick around long enough to hear them say how beautiful you are, but not long enough to let on that you care what they think.

The only exception to these rules is when the visitor is a confirmed cat-hater. That's when you need to pull out all the stops – purr, rub, cling and cuddle, until the offending human sneezes and departs abruptly.

When you have your human all to yourself again, fix her with an adoring gaze and purr like a well-tuned Ferrari.

When you need to get out of a bad situation, like claw clipping, a bath or a trip to the vet's, first look at your human with slightly crossed eyes and give her a silent meow. If that doesn't work, howl loudly and show your claws. If your human is well-read, it may help to quote Thoreau on civil disobedience.

When all else fails and you find yourself locked in the kitty carrier and heading for the highway, sing protest songs all the way to the doctor's office.

FAITH: Bonding with humans is as easy as catching a catnip mouse, if my adopted mother is any indication. Getting along with other felines, however, requires tact, subtlety and a wide range of communication skills. Fortunately, I'm a diplomat by *purr*-fession. In my smartly tailored gray suit, I even look like one.

As a newcomer, I had to carve out my territory gradually. At first, Mom confined me to a small bathroom so the other cats could get used to my sounds and scent. This was mostly for Cleo's benefit. I already knew Hope because we're littermates, but she'd been in the hospital, so it had been a while since I'd seen her.

The first rule of feline diplomacy is never to surrender an advantage once you gain one. During the couple of weeks I spent in that little room, I discovered it had its benefits, including a litter box that was just my size, curtained off for privacy, and a high window with a wonderful view of all the places I used to prowl when I was feral. I claimed that litter box and window, and they've been mine ever since.

Once I had the whole apartment to explore, there were new challenges to meet. Cleo was willing to tolerate me as a member of her entourage, but only if I obeyed her without question – "Yes, Your Majesty" – and flattered her outrageously. Hope was OK most of the time. She has a good heart under all that fluff, but she's bigger than me and would play too rough. Sometimes she had me pinned before I even knew a wrestling match had been scheduled.

It didn't take me long to figure out the best way to treat each cat. I continued to obey and flatter Cleo, but also added some new moves. When she was resting, I'd lie beside her and give her my most affectionate purrs. When she groomed herself, I'd offer to help. When Mom passed out snacks, I'd let Cleo have the first bite. When we played games, I'd let her win.

Like most friendships worth keeping, ours took a while to develop, but now Cleo treats me like her best buddy and says I can stop calling her "Your Highness." Sometimes we even sleep together.

Hope required a distinctly different approach. There's no diplomatic way to say this: Sometimes she simply got too big for her britches and needed to be taken down a peg. I explained to her that dinner is a first-come, first-served affair and she could just wait her turn. I participate actively in games, play to win and refuse to let her hog all the glory. Finally, I've learned how to deal with those surprise wrestling matches. I act submissive until Hope thinks she's won, then bite her on the leg and chase her up the cat tree.

Although I've become a well-adjusted member of a multi-cat family, I still can't see why Mom keeps those other girls around. As I've told her many times, I'm all the cat she needs.

HOPE: I don't mean to be insensitive and I hope Cleo will forgive me, but competing for attention with a spoiled Siamese princess can be very stressful. Sometimes I feel as if I'm wrestling for my self-esteem.

As a "demo-cat," I believe in equality, not monarchy, but Cleo always insists on having the upper paw. To live with her without losing my dignity, I have to be constantly on the lookout for ways to upstage her. If it were up to Cleo, the spotlight would follow her eternally. I'd never get my 15 minutes of fame, or even five minutes to bask in the sunbeams on the balcony.

Playing Bette Davis to this feline Joan Crawford requires all the ingenuity that I can muster. Let's say we both think Mom has been working too long.

I jump on the computer monitor and lie there, patting Mom on the forehead. Before I can even get a nuzzle in return, there's Cleo, walking across the keyboard to spell out, "Hi, Mom! Let's play" or "Isn't it time for lunch?"

It's not as if I can't spell, either. My paws are just too big to hit one key at a time, and I refuse to embarrass myself by writing gibberish.

At night, I try to be the first one to bed so I can lie on my back, wave my paws, wiggle my whiskers and generally look so adorable that I'll be the center of attention. But the moment Mom lies down, Cleo sits on her stomach to obscure the view or kneads her arm to keep her from petting any other kitties who happen to be in the vicinity.

Well, I *purr*-severed and finally found a solution. The only time Cleo isn't demanding attention is when she's asleep, so I learned how to hypnotize her. Now when I want Mom all to myself, I simply wave a yo-yo back and forth in front of Cleo's face while chanting, "Sleepy cat, sleepy cat." Within seconds she's deep in dreamland and I can be queen for a day.

I was going to add something about reasoning with a cat, but I'm not sure that's possible. When you want a kitty to do your bidding, it's best to skip the small talk and bring out the bribes.

To stop a family feud, simply throw warm, freshly dried laundry on the bed. The feline foes will forget their differences and frolic together like kittens.

To coax a cat into a carrier, toss in a tasty treat and close the door the moment the kitty follows it in.

❖ ❖ ❖

To maneuver a puss into position for a bath or flea treatment, offer a favorite toy or treat. (Shrimp, which can double as Frisbees, fall into both categories.) The idea is to captivate the cat so he won't notice the running water or vial of goo. If you ever have to give a cat a pill, forgo the formalities. Simply open her mouth, toss it down her throat, and make up for the indignity with plenty of treats and strokes after the fact.

❖ ❖ ❖

Excuse my yawn. I'm getting awfully tired all of a sudden.

Hope, give me that yo-yo!

CATS AND THE STARS

Astrological Guidance for the New Millennium

Like any important relationship, a human-feline partnership has a head start if the personalities are astrologically compatible.

People and cats of different astrological signs have distinctive traits that make them better matches for some individuals than for others. For example, a quiet Virgo person who likes to spend evenings curled up with a good book would prefer a Taurus or Cancer cat who's content to sit by the fire to an Aries one who's constantly dashing here and there with great energy. On the other paw, the Aries cat wants a human companion who will devote lots of time to active play sessions. A Leo or Aquarius would be a good choice.

If you're about to adopt a cat (or a human), you can use this information to find one who's likely to suit your personality and lifestyle. If you already have a cat (or a human), you can use your new astrological knowledge to increase mutual understanding and find ways to make life with each other more harmonious.

A cat's astrological sign can intensify or modify the breed characteristics mentioned in the second chapter. Any Turkish Van will enjoy playing in water, but one born under Pisces might want to swim laps in an Olympic-sized pool. Any Russian Blue will be somewhat reserved, but one born under Libra will be quicker than most to make friends.

Unless you adopted your cat from a breeder, or sneaked a peek at your human's birth certificate, you may not know the exact date he or she was born. If you know only the month, read about the two signs that might apply and choose the one that suits your puss or person better.

We apologize in advance for presenting this information mostly from the human point of view. This is not out of any desire to slight our feline readers. It's just that the humans are the ones who need the most guidance.

Stray and feral cats usually show great wisdom in making their adoption decisions, and hapless kitties who end up with the wrong people usually vote with their paws by taking off in search of better homes.

ARIES
(MAR. 21–APR. 19)

Symbol: The Ram
Planetary ruler: Mars
Element: Cardinal fire
Greatest desire: Discovery
Best day: Tuesday

Aries Human: You're a hard-charging doer who's constantly on the go, following your latest enthusiasm wherever it leads. Before you adopt a cat, ask yourself if you can spare enough time to give her the high-quality companionship she deserves. If you think you can, but know you're going to be away from home for long periods some days, adopt a pair of pusses who can keep each other company. You love the antics of kittens, but an older cat or cats would make a better choice if you're unable to take "kitty parent leave" to ease their transition into your home.

Aries Cat: If there were a feline Olympics, this cat would be a contender. Bright, inquisitive and into everything, the demanding Aries feline is like the television detective Columbo with fur. Just when you think she's had enough food, playtime or cuddling, she comes back and lays a paw on your arm as if to say, "Excuse me, there's one more thing..."

When Aries wants affection, she'll let you know by butting her head against you in imitation of her symbolic Ram. This high-maintenance cat needs a true companion, not just a caretaker – she wants (and, in fact, needs) to bond with you emotionally. She may fit in

68

comfortably with a large family, but she'll always have a favorite person.

Aries is totally fearless, so you'll have to supply the caution. She should never be allowed outside unless she's in a carrier or on a leash. Make sure she wears her tag for identification. And it's wise to add a tattoo or microchip in case she loses her collar.

Best Matches: Leo, Sagittarius or Aquarius human

TAURUS
(APR. 20–MAY 20)

Symbol: The Bull
Planetary ruler: Venus
Element: Fixed earth
Greatest desire: Pleasure
Best day: Friday

Taurus Human: Members of your sign are incurable animal lovers, but you'll expect your feline pal to adapt to you rather than the other way around. You have strong territorial urges of your own and won't take kindly to a cat who claims your favorite easy chair and refuses to consider time-sharing. Resistant to change, you'll want the cat to eat and sleep when you do. If he agrees to abide by a few rules of the house, though, you won't mind handing out tasty treats and providing a velvet cushion for him to rest on. You'll enjoy many agreeable evenings at home in front of the TV.

Taurus Cat: The Taurus cat rules his human with an iron paw in a velvet glove. As a child of Venus, he's full of purrs and eager to please, but it must be on his terms. When he wants to cuddle, surrender gracefully or he'll sit on your head. When he's off doing important cat business, be understanding and let him sleep.

Taurus is the gourmet among cats, so one of the best ways you can show your affection is to offer him a place by your side at mealtimes and a bite of anything he wants to sample. Favorites are rare roast beef, shrimp in garlic sauce and roast turkey breast, but don't be surprised if Taurus also wants to try asparagus, apples or ice cream.

A loving companion for the entire family, Taurus usually chooses one special bedtime buddy. If it's you, don't shut the bedroom door and break his heart. Instead, think how lucky you are to have a furry heating pad.

Best Matches: Cancer, Pisces or Capricorn human

GEMINI
(MAY 21–JUNE 21)

Symbol: The Twins
Planetary ruler: Mercury
Element: Mutable air
Greatest desire: Self-expression
Best day: Wednesday

Gemini Human: Bright, friendly and playful, you need a cat who shares these characteristics and will mix well with your pals by the dozens who are always around. Adopt a young kitten who's active, outgoing and curious, and she should grow up to be an adaptable party animal who'll be happy to help you entertain at home or even accompany you on vacation. Before you adopt, ask yourself if you can set aside daily quality time that's just for you and your cat. No matter how much a kitty companion may enjoy sharing your social life, she'll want to know you think she's special.

Gemini Cat: This kitty would make an excellent talk show host. She won't wait to speak until she has something important to say but will offer an opinion about anything, and she enjoys small talk as much as a serious conversation. You can encourage her by replying in her language; she may return the favor by saying a few words in yours.

Bright and active, Gemini needs a variety of stimulating games to keep her pouncing, chasing and investigating. Give her plenty of bags and boxes to explore, along with more sophisticated kitty toys like a remote-controlled mouse to hunt. She also likes to bat at things, so offer her a ball attached to a coiled wire in a carpeted base, or a feathery toy on a wand that "flies" when you wave it.

For Gemini, kittenhood lasts forever. A member of this sign makes a great companion for a child who needs a playmate who can match his or her energy level.

Best Matches: Libra, Aquarius or Aries human

CANCER
(JUNE 22–JULY 22)

Symbol: The Crab
Planetary ruler: Moon
Element: Cardinal water
Greatest desire: Happy home life
Best day: Monday

Cancer Human: Yours is the sign of nurturing, but if you're constantly taking care of human loved ones, you may not have much energy left over to care for a kitty as well. You think cats are attractive and entertaining and will gladly share your home with one, as long as he stays where you want him to and doesn't annoy you by begging for treats, jumping on your lap when you're busy or trying to share your bed. Before you adopt a cat, ask yourself if you can take time to provide him with the toys he needs to fend off boredom and the affection he needs to be happy. If not, get a plant.

Cancer Cat: This kitty can really make a house feel like a home – if you ask him politely, he may even let you share it. Thoroughly domestic, he'll claim the comfiest napping spots, help you sort the laundry and find a perch in the kitchen where he can watch you prepare his meals. He's not demanding, but may sulk if he feels you're not paying him enough attention. Once neutered, he's unlikely to stray. In fact, you may need a special long-handled broom to sweep him out from under the bed when it's time to visit the doctor, or even the pet toy store.

If you're not quite sure that your cat is a Cancer, wait

until the night of the next Full Moon. If this is truly his sign, your normally quiet kitty will display his lunar influence by dashing madly around the house, chasing things that you can't see, and either howling soulfully or singing like Paw-varotti. Fortunately, when the sun comes up the next morning, your well-behaved companion will return.

Best Matches: Taurus, Virgo or Pisces human

LEO
(JULY 23–AUG. 22)

Symbol: The Lion
Planetary ruler: The Sun
Element: Fixed fire
Greatest desire: Appreciation
Best day: Sunday

Leo Human: Your home is your castle and you can be bossy to the other people there, yet you melt at the sight of a helpless kitten who needs you in so many ways. Once you accept the little one as part of the family, you'll treat her as you do your human children, spoiling her and catering to her every whim. Your only flaw as a feline companion is that you may expect your kitty to become a cat show champion or even appear as a spokescat in a TV commercial. Resist the urge to be a stage mother. If your puss has her heart set on Hollywood, she'll let you know.

Leo Cat: When you share your home with a Leo cat, there's no doubt who's in charge – and it's not you. This cat's expressive gestures and panther-like grace set her apart as nature's royalty, whether she descended from a long line of grand champions or just strolled in from the alley. She'll show her love by walking all over you (literally) and expecting to be included in all your activities. When your plans don't include her, she'll be reasonable, as long as you take time to tell her how splendid and cherished she is. Remember, even royals have occasional attacks of insecurity.

True to her astrological heritage, the Leo cat loves sunshine. Create a safe, sunny spot for her on a screened porch, balcony or window box. You can buy one of the latter that's designed to let urban felines bask safely. This kitty won't even want to sleep in darkness, so let her bed down near a soft reading light, or wait until she's asleep to turn off yours.

Best Matches: Leo, Sagittarius or Aries human

VIRGO

(AUG. 23–SEPT. 22)

Symbol: The Maiden
Planetary ruler: Mercury
Element: Mutable earth
Greatest desire: Order
Best day: Wednesday

Virgo Human: Your sign is associated with small domestic animals, and cats are probably your favorites. Neat, tidy and well-organized yourself, you appreciate the feline's cleanliness and desire for a regular routine. You won't even mind an occasional display of finickiness

– after all, you're pretty particular about what you eat. When you adopt a cat, you let him know the ground rules and expect him to obey them. If he does anything out of the ordinary, you're on the phone to the vet in a flash. Stop worrying. Tolerate your kitty's quirks and hope he'll show you the same courtesy.

Virgo Cat: Like his human counterparts, the Virgo cat believes in an orderly universe and wants to do his part to keep things running smoothly. Unlike those lazy pusses who give felines a bad name, Virgo wants a job to do, so let him serve as your alarm clock, tell you when the litter box needs cleaning or call the family to dinner. Play games that challenge him to do better each time.

Most cats spend about a third of their waking hours grooming themselves. Virgo the *purr*-fectionist spends as much time as a model preparing for a photo layout. He'll even welcome help from you. Stroke him with a grooming glove for a few minutes every day and take him to a groomer for a bath, conditioner and cream rinse a couple of times a year.

Affectionate but self-reliant, Virgo does well as an only cat and doesn't mind being alone when you're at work, as long as you show him plenty of affection when you return.

Best Matches: Taurus, Cancer or Capricorn human

LIBRA
(SEPT. 23–OCT. 23)

Symbol: The Scales
Planetary ruler: Venus
Element: Cardinal air
Greatest desire: Harmony
Best day: Friday

Libra Human: You may adopt a cat for her beauty, but end up appreciating her for the years of love and friendship she provides. Members of your sign like constant companionship. If you're single, adopting a cat or two for company can keep you from marrying too soon or taking an unsuitable human roommate just so you won't be alone. If you choose a purebred who turns out to be an excellent example of her breed, the two of you can have lots of fun going to cat shows. Who knows? Your glamour puss might even introduce you to your attractive, cat-loving, future mate.

Libra Cat: The Libra cat doesn't see any reason for the distinctions made here, since she's convinced that she's a human baby. She wants her own place at the dining room table, her own pillow on your bed and an active role in your social evenings. She'll gladly learn tricks to entertain your friends, as long as they remember to tell her how remarkable she is.

Gentle and cuddly, Libra loves to be bathed, groomed and fitted for a fancy collar – anything to be a pretty kitty. She won't mind when your kids dress her up, as long as the outfits are becoming.

Libras often have that special combination of good looks,

elegance and charm that wins blue ribbons in competition. If your kitty seems willing, take her to a cat show just once (there are plenty for mixed breeds as well as purebreds) and you may discover you have a rising star. Even if she doesn't come home with a prize, she'll revel in all the extra attention.

Best Matches: Gemini, Leo or Libra human

SCORPIO
(OCT. 24–NOV. 21)

Symbol: The Scorpion
Planetary ruler: Pluto
Element: Fixed water
Greatest desire: Power
Best day: Tuesday

Scorpio Human: Always striving for mastery and control in the outside world, you become a different, more relaxed person when you're at home. Your cat may be one of the few companions who gets to see your gentle, vulnerable side. When you adopt a kitty, you consider it a serious commitment and expect devotion and loyalty in return for the affection and nurturing you provide. Whether or not you're physically demonstrative, you'll form a strong bond with your cat and commune with him telepathically. Why not? He's the most reliable psychic you know.

Scorpio Cat: Like power-hungry Salem on the TV sitcom *Sabrina, The Teenage Witch*, Scorpio cats occasionally dream of taking over the world, but most can be happy just taking charge of a household, acting as watch-cats and keeping the family secrets. Your Scorpio kitty will have some secrets of his own, too. If you don't want to lose money and valuables, keep your wallet or purse beyond the reach of his thieving paw. If you don't want him making unauthorized midnight prowls, double-check the locks on all doors and windows before you turn in for the night.

This cat is an intelligent and loving companion, but an intensely possessive one. If you have other pets, greet Scorpio first when you return home, or he'll walk off in a jealous huff.

Intuitive and psychic, especially where your safety is concerned, the Scorpio kitty will warn you in case of danger and bravely rescue everyone he can if there's an emergency.

Best Matches: Cancer, Capricorn or Pisces human

SAGITTARIUS
(NOV. 22–DEC. 21)

Symbol: The Archer
Planetary ruler: Jupiter
Element: Mutable fire
Greatest desire: Adventure
Best day: Thursday

Sagittarius Human: With your humor, optimism and interest in others' welfare, you're a delightful companion for a friend of any species. You tend to be absent-minded, though, so you may not be too dependable. If you adopt a cat, you need to be aware of her special needs and be willing to provide for them on a regular schedule, since felines are creatures of routine. She'll want food, water and a clean litter box twice a day, her claws trimmed every other week and flea prevention once a month. Meet those needs and you and your kitty can be great playmates for each other.

Sagittarius Cat: It's said that Jupiter brings his children luck, and it's a good thing, because adventurous Sagittarius needs all the help she can get to stay out of trouble. Friendly, adventurous, restless and reckless, this kitty will take off on a whim to investigate a scent or follow a new feline or human neighbor who seems to be doing something interesting.

When your Sagittarian kitty is three or four months old, try training her to walk with you on a leash. If she's willing, you can have daily outdoor adventures together without risking losing her. Still, she should carry as much identification as possible at all times, just in case. Double-check locks when you're indoors together, and stay alert in case she learns how to use a doorknob.

Sagittarius is a mighty hunter, so offer her chances to "kill" furry toys and chase fake prey during playtime. This will eliminate unsightly trophies and give the neighborhood wildlife a chance.

Best Matches: Aries, Sagittarius or Aquarius human

CAPRICORN
(DEC. 22–JAN. 19)

Symbol: The Goat
Planetary ruler: Saturn
Element: Cardinal earth
Greatest desire: Recognition
Best day: Saturday

Capricorn Human: You and your cat can be very good for each other. He'll remind you that there are more important things than slaying corporate dragons, and you'll give him a sense of security and excellent care. When you come home weary from a hard day at work, let your kitty purr on your lap – it'll give you both feelings of belonging and contentment. And you get the benefit of having your blood pressure lowered. The only feline trait that may throw you is unpredictability. You want to know exactly what to expect, but as your cat will show you, this is neither possible nor as much fun as spontaneity.

Capricorn Cat: Old beyond his years, Capricorn seems to have the wisdom of an ancient sage from early kittenhood. Bright enough to learn from experience, he'll watch from the sidelines while other pets engage in various forms of mischief, and avoid the ones that lead to danger or scoldings. Operating on a basis of mutual respect, he wants to know you approve of him as well as love him.

This kitty thinks obedience school is such a great idea that he will gladly take you there. He wants a human he can count on for regular meals, grooming and play sessions. He's a creature of habit, so any changes to his schedule should be made gradually.

When it's time to play, Capricorn loves a ball game, as long as you agree to fetch. When he thinks another cat is getting too much attention, he'll drop his dignity and perform the most outrageous stunts to reclaim center stage.

Best Matches: Taurus, Virgo or Scorpio human

AQUARIUS
(JAN. 20–FEB. 18)

Symbol: The Water Bearer
Planetary ruler: Uranus
Element: Fixed air
Greatest desire: Independence
Best day: Saturday

Aquarius Human: You appreciate cats because they have minds of their own, just like you. Independent to a fault, you prefer another self-reliant creature as a companion. You're not stingy with affection, but you don't want anyone, feline or otherwise, begging for your attention 24 hours a day. You're happy to grant your kitty occasional solitude in exchange for some of your own. When you're feeling sociable and invite the gang over for a party, don't let your puss get lost in the shuffle. Move her food and water bowls to a quiet corner of the house where she can get away from it all.

Aquarius Cat: An agreeable loner, the Aquarius kitty makes friends with everyone but keeps much of herself to herself. Adept at getting along with family members of all species, she'll form a special bond with each individual, but want time alone to think her catty thoughts. She's not a lap cat, but she'll show her affection by lying by your side and purring, and doing household security patrols.

It's best to turn off the computer and hide the remote control when Aquarius appears on the scene. She likes high-tech gadgets as much as human Aquarians do, and she'll find new uses for them if you let her. Remotes are fun to skate on, and stereo cables are great for predator practice.

Super-bright and able to learn almost anything fast, Aquarius will delight you with her antics. She planned it that way, hoping you'd forgive her for kicking her litter outside the box, being a messy eater and keeping a schedule that's erratic, even for a cat.

Best Matches: Gemini, Sagittarius or Aries human

PISCES
(FEB. 19–MAR. 20)

Symbol: The Fishes
Planetary ruler: Neptune
Element: Mutable water
Greatest desire: Unity
Best day: Thursday

Pisces Human: The ultimate cat co-dependent, you take to feline companionship like a fish takes to water. You're highly sensitive to the vibrations of those you spend the most time with. If it's your cats (Pisces seldom settles for just one), you're likely to find yourself meowing, purring and getting silly at the slightest whiff of catnip. It's no wonder kitties easily accept you as one of their own. If you want to be accepted as top cat, remember to exude authority as well as affection with your feline friends. You'd hate it if they made you wear a collar and eat off the floor.

Pisces Cat: Devoted, sensitive and empathetic, the Pisces cat senses that it's his job to keep the family together. He'll bond with everyone and likes to see all his humans gathered in the same room. If you're his favorite, this kitty will become literally attached to you, nestling in your lap, riding on your shoulders and napping behind your knees. Pisces wouldn't think of sleeping anywhere but by your side, so move over and let his soothing purrs send you off to dreamland.

This offbeat kitty sometimes seems vague or distant – meditating, lost in a favorite piece of music, playing with imaginary friends or chasing something that isn't there. But he reads your mind and moods and is the first to offer comfort when you're ill, worried or feeling down.

When it comes to recreation, Pisces is more of an observer than active participant. He doesn't need too many toys or formal play sessions as long as he has his family to entertain him.

Best Matches: Cancer, Scorpio or Capricorn human

AMAZING CATS

Fascinating "Tails" and True Stories

Venerated as gods, used in spells, regarded as good luck charms or reviled as witches' helpers, cats have been seen throughout history as creatures of mystery and magic with mystical powers beyond human comprehension.

Cats in Myths, Legend and Religion

❖ The ancient Egyptians worshipped the cat-headed goddess Bastet, who symbolized fertility, motherliness and feminine grace. They treated their feline companions with great affection and respect, making it a capital offense to kill one. When cats died, they were laid to rest with ceremony. Archaeologists have unearthed thousands of cat mummies, accompanied by mummified mice, presumably to keep the cats snacking happily on their way to the afterlife.

❖ In South America, some people worshipped a puma god and thought medicine men turned into jaguars when they died.

❖ The Greeks credited their goddess Artemis with creating the cat and ascending to the moon in feline form.

The Romans gave Venus, their goddess of love, many of the attributes of Bastet and often depicted her with a cat. Some historians believe importing cats to England was the Romans' greatest contribution toward civilizing the British.

For transportation, the Norse fertility goddess Freya used a cat-drawn chariot. Finnish people thought the souls of the dead were collected by cats drawing a sled.

When people in Java wanted to make it rain, they would bathe two cats, a male and a female, then carry them in a procession with music.

In France, where cats were thought to be keepers of the corn spirit, they were decked out with ribbons, flowers and ears of corn to ensure a fruitful harvest. When the reaping was done, cats were again adorned and taken to celebratory feasts and dances. A French legend says that cats are the only beings who know the path back to the Garden of Eden.

A South African tribe told of a cat who served as the "external soul" for an entire family whose lives depended on her existence. When she died, the family members quickly fell lifeless, too.

A Hungarian superstition claims that all cats become witches between the ages of seven and 12 unless tattooed with the sign of the cross soon after birth. (I'm not all that worried about Cleo getting witchier with age. As far as I can tell, she's been casting love spells all along.)

In Japan, a cat with a raised left paw brings wealth, while one with its right paw raised brings luck and happiness.

❖ The legend about the origin of Oriental astrology says that shortly before leaving this world, Buddha invited all the animals to a feast. Two felines, the tiger and the cat (sometimes called rabbit), were among the 12 who responded and were rewarded by having the Zodiac signs named after them. The tiger, full of yang energy, is said to represent courage and zest for life; the cat, his ying counterpart, symbolizes peacefulness, luck and longevity.

❖ Western astrology, like the ancient Egyptian culture, associates its one feline sign, Leo the Lion, with the sun.

❖ Felines appear on six cards in the Tarot deck. There are heraldic lions on the thrones of the King and Queen of Wands (the queen also has a smiling black cat at her feet), and sphinxes with women's heads and panthers' bodies on The Chariot. There is a lion being tamed by a woman on Strength, and lions also appear on The Wheel of Fortune and The World.

❖ Cats have often been associated with clairvoyance. An early European tradition held that one could acquire this gift by growing up with a tortoiseshell kitty.

❖ Hindus, who revere all living creatures, have a special rule about cats: Each faithful family is expected to house and feed one.

❖ Islamic lore includes many tales about the prophet Mohammed and his beloved cats. One story tells how a considerate cat saved the prophet from death by snakebite. Another tells of Mohammed's kindness in cutting off the sleeve of his robe rather than disturb Muezza, the cat who was sleeping on it. (She said thanks by sharing her special powers with the prophet.)

❖ Cats have guarded temples in Thailand and other parts of Asia for centuries. One Thai legend says that highly spiritual people reincarnate as cats as their last stage on the way to heaven. Another explains the dark patches on the shoulders of some Siamese cats as "temple marks" left by Buddha's fingers when he touched them in blessing.

❖ The Talmud praises feline cleanliness. The Bible contains only one, neutral mention of a cat (as opposed to larger felines like lions). In the Old Testament Book of Baruch (in the Catholic Bible), in a passage warning against idols, the fact that cats walk on these graven images is given as one proof that the statues can't be divine.

❖ Despite calling Jesus "the Lion of Judah" and using the lion to symbolize the Gospel of St. Mark, Christianity has not always treated cats kindly. St. Gertrude of Nivelles was associated with cats and St. Francis of Assisi became known as the champion of all creatures. Nevertheless, night-prowling felines somehow came to be associated with the devil and witches, and a host of cruel practices arose in the name of banishing evil.

❖ After cats started killing plague-bearing rats during the Middle Ages, they began to return to the good graces of European Christians. Popes Leo XII and Pius IX and Cardinal Richelieu were only three of many cat-loving pillars of the Church.

❖ Catty superstitions persist to this day. Americans believe white cats are lucky and black cats unlucky, while Britons think the reverse is true. Professional gamblers everywhere believe that caring for cats and treating them well will increase their luck. (Cats probably started this rumor in order to increase the number of good homes available to them.)

Real-Life Super Cats

As interesting as legends and superstitions about felines may be, we agree with Oscar Wilde, who said, "The mystery of life is in the visible, not the invisible." The truth about cats is often even more amazing than the tall tales.

Take cats' psychic abilities, for instance. Long the stuff of folklore, they've been verified in a number of 20th-century scientific experiments. Some of the best-known are J.B. Rhine's at Duke University in Durham, N.C., in 1950. His results suggested strongly that cats can predict danger that threatens them or their people, foretell their humans' unexpected return, find their way back home after being lost and use psychic abilities to find their people more than 30 miles away in places where they've never been.

While some cats' "predictions" can be explained as nothing more than acute hearing or excellent timing, psychic pusses have also scored high on ESP tests in which these special senses play no part.

The homing instinct seems to be especially strong in older cats released within 12 km (7½ mi.) of home. Yet there are confirmed cases of cats psi-trailing their owners to new homes hundreds, even thousands of miles away. One of the most amazing is the story of a New York veterinarian who found a new home for his cat rather than subject it to the long trip to California, where he was moving. Months later, a cat that looked just like his former companion, complete with a distinctive bump on its tail that left no room for doubt, showed up at his new West Coast house.

Female cats are rightly praised as exceptional mothers, but the male of the species has a bad reputation that's mostly undeserved, as far as I can tell. It's said that tomcats either take no interest in kittens, or, worse, get jealous and attack them. The feral toms in my neighborhood certainly don't act that way.

When last seen, Charlie – Faith's and Hope's brother – was doing a great job as big brother to his mom's new litter, leading them to food or shelter when he could see she needed a rest. Mr. Fur-bottom – Hope's father – dropped by frequently to check on her when she first came to live with me. Mr. Panther – Faith's father (and maybe Charlie's) – still keeps an eye out for Faith on his nightly patrols of the neighborhood. She watches for him from her window. He also took Charlie on male-bonding outings until Charlie found a home.

An intriguing catty tradition holds that you shouldn't name a kitty, just stay alert and wait for him to name himself. While we wouldn't want to spoil the fun of people like the bishop who named his little spitfire "Lucy Fur," or the Southern belle who dubbed her loudly purring giant "Magnolia Thunderpussy," some cats do proclaim their names in no uncertain terms. I wouldn't believe it if I hadn't met two highly psychic kitties who did just that.

One night, more than 20 years ago, I was on my way home from a killer day at work, with no thought but to stumble in and head for bed. But something told me to stop at the supermarket. Once inside, the same something told me to buy tuna – and milk, which I don't even drink.

When I arrived home, I found a half-starved, half-grown kitten on my doorstep, crying loudly. Understanding immediately that I'd bought the tuna and milk for this stranger, I put down a bowl of each and watched the youngster inhale them both in record time. Then her cries began again.

Before dinner and afterward, the kitty sang her name loudly: "Maaaaao, Maaaaao." And so began my long and happy association with Chairman Mao, my first cat.

Years later, a friend's cat had kittens and she offered me one. Being catless at the time, I agreed. Spirit, the mother, was a lovely Oriental Shorthair and I'd seen her litter briefly, but not knowing what my particular kitty looked like, or what I'd name him, I set a date to stop by my friend's house to get better acquainted.

It wasn't necessary. A few hours later, a beautiful black, green-eyed kitten appeared in my mind's eye, saying "I am Star, son of Spirit." Star turned out to be the perfect name for this kitty, who was solid black except for a white star on his chest.

As among people, some cats are more spiritually evolved than others. Several of my departed feline friends have shown up in dreams and visions. One even perched on my shoulder in ghostly form the day after he died – and gave me a glimpse of kitty heaven.

Those who laugh at the notion of feline spirituality are welcome to explain this:

I was out for a walk late one night last year when I saw two tomcats having a serious street fight, somersaulting through the air until the fur flew. "Kitties," I called out in what I hoped was an authoritative voice, "God says we should love one another." Imagine my amazement when the cats immediately separated, then walked off side by side, tails crossed in friendship.

CLAWSSARY

The following terms, both factual and fanciful, are sure to spice up your catty conversations:

A

Agouti: Hairs with bands of several shades, like those of the Abyssinian and Singapura

Ailurophile: Cat lover

Ailurophobe: Person who's scared of felines; what a cat would call a fraidy-human

B

Brachycephalic: With an abnormally short nose and flattened face, like some Persians

Breed standard: Description of the ideal cat of a certain breed. Totaling 100 points for dozens of factors from color of eyes to length of tail, it's the basis for grading purebreds in show competition.

C

Cataclysm: Earth tremor caused by cats stamping their feet around an empty food bowl

Catacomb: Fluffy's grooming aid

Catalyst: Written reminder of essentials to buy, like cat food, turkey, tuna

Catamaran: Anything a cat can pounce on to deliver her from the tub at bath time

Catamite: What makes kitty's ear itch

Catamount: The best portion of anything

Catapult: Special pounce that propels cats to the tops of bookcases and refrigerators

Catastrophe: Running out of kitty litter; see Mewspaper

Catcall: Director's way of inviting feline actors to audition for roles

Catechism: Kitty's prayer book

Category: Trophy your prowler leaves on the doorstep

Caterwaul: Where tomcats gather to serenade the ladies

Cat fancy: People who breed, register, show or simply admire felines

Catfish: Anything fresh and expensive, like salmon filets or swordfish steaks

Catnip: Love bite from an exuberant feline

Cat's cradle: Behind the knees of a friendly, reclining human

Catskills: Feline talents

Catwalk: Cattitude in motion

Cat and mouse: Favorite computer game

CFA: Cat Fanciers' Association. The world's largest feline registry, it's 97 years old and based in North America.

Chinchilla: A white coat tipped with black, often seen in Persians

Claws and effect: Kitty karma

Clawstrophobia: Fear of manicures

Cool cat: This sounds like a feline who's hip to the latest trends, but in breeder's terminology it's a kitty whose coat is a cool color like silver or blue.

D

Dominant gene: Genetic trait that when carried is always expressed

Down hair: Soft, insulating hair in undercoat

E

ESP: Extrasensory purrception, a cat's sixth sense that enables him to complete nine lives

F

Felinity: The essence of cattiness, synonym for Purrfection

Flehmen response: Lifting the lip, creating an expression that looks like a sneer but is actually a cat's way of getting a better fix on a scent

Furball: The main event on the feline social calendar

Furnish: To decorate carpet, couch and chairs by shedding hairs of opposite hue

Furtive: Cat in a seafood market

G

Gauntlets: White hind paws on a colored cat

Ghost markings: Faint tabby markings sometimes seen in the coats of solid-colored kittens

Guard hairs: Long, coarse hairs that protect the undercoat and aid in waterproofing

H

Hisstory: Account of a catfight

Hock: The feline ankle

Hot: Reddish coat colors

J

Jacobson's organ: A sensory organ in the cat's nasal cavity that analyzes tastes as well as smells

K

King of beasts: The lion, or any tomcat who wins your heart

Kitten cap: Underlying color seen on the heads of some white kittens. It fades with age.

Kitty corner: The section of a room that offers the most comfortable furniture

Kvetch: Complain about going to the doctor

L

Leap year: From age two to three, when cats perfect their high jumps

Litterature: Restroom reading matter

Locket: Medallion of white hair on the chest of a colored cat

M

Mascara lines: A cat's natural makeup, dark Cleopatra-like lines extending from the outer corners of the eyes

Mewseum: Institution that houses the works of great artists, like Pawcasso and Mirow

Mewspaper: Too depressing to read, but sanitary enough to shred for emergency litter box filler

Mink: A combination of pointed and sepia patterns commonly seen in Tonkinese

Mittens: White forepaws on a colored cat

N

Nictitating membrane: A thin third eyelid, situated below the eye near its inner corner, that acts as a protective mechanism when a cat senses a danger to its eyes

Nose stop: A change in direction seen in profile at the top of a cat's nose, also called a nose break

O

Octopuss: Eight-kitten litter

Odd eyes: Not strange, just of different colors. A white Angora or Persian, for example, sometimes has one blue eye and one gold.

P

Pawtucket: Explanation for the disappearance of any shiny object

Pedigree: A purebred's family tree

Polydactyl: A cat with at least six toes on each front foot and five on each rear one – more than enough to give you paws

Purrcentage: The lion's share

Purrchase: Game of tag

Purrcolate: Make coffee

Purrfection: *See* Felinity

Purrfume: The scent of a freshly washed kitty

Purrgatory: Where naughty cats go to be purrfected

Purrpetuity: Living happily ever after

Purrple: Cats' favorite color

Purrsistence: The ability to wangle all the treats you want

Purrspective: The view from a sunny window

Pussibilities: Candidates for adoption

Pussport: Where you dock your catamaran

Puss in Boots: Cat making a winter fashion statement

Q

Queen: A cat having kittens, or any female cat that wins your heart

R

Random breeding: Choosing one's own mate without the help of a breeder

Recessive gene: A genetic characteristic that is present but not expressed

Refurbish: Fill in bald spots, as with Rogaine

Rexing: A mutation causing a curly coat

Ruff: Longer fur, reminiscent of a lion's mane, that appears on the neck and chest of some cats

S

Scent marking: Marking territory with urine or scent from facial glands

Selective breeding: The feline equivalent of an arranged marriage

Self: Coat of one color

Sepia: Dark color on a cat's extremities, shading to a lighter tone of the same color on its body

Smoke: Colored coat with white undercoat

Spectacles: Bands of white or lighter hair around a cat's eyes

T

Tabby: Pattern of stripes or patches nature invented to protect cats in the wild, dominant among purebreds and random-breds alike. Its most distinctive characteristic is the big "M" on a cat's forehead, like the one that gave TV star Morris his name.

Trivial purrsuit: Chasing a gnat

Turkey trot: Race to the Thanksgiving table

U

Undercoat: Layer of insulating fur under the topcoat, common in breeds like the Maine Coon that originated in cold climates

V

Van: Pattern of color on the head and tail only

Vomeronasal organ: Same as Jacobson's organ

Vowels: Scientists' name for meows

W

Wool: Smart cats pull this over their humans' eyes all the time; some Siamese also like to snack on it.

Z

Zen: The art of living contentedly in the present, this is the natural state of consciousness for cats and can be learned by contemplating your kitty.